Skills *in*
RATIONAL EMOTIVE
BEHAVIOUR
Counselling & Psychotherapy

Series editor: Francesca Inskipp

Skills in Counselling & Psychotherapy is a new series of practical guides for trainees and practitioners. Each book takes one of the main approaches to therapeutic work and describes the core skills and techniques used within that approach.

Topics covered include

♦ how to assess the suitability of the approach for the client
♦ how to establish and develop the therapeutic relationship
♦ how to help the client change.

This is the first series of books to look at skills specific to the different theoretical approaches, making it ideal for use on a range of courses which prepare the trainees to work directly with clients.

Books in the series:

Skills in Gestalt Counselling & Psychotherapy
Phil Joyce & Charlotte Sills

Skills in Transactional Analysis Counselling & Psychotherapy
Christine Lister-Ford

Skills in Person-Centred Counselling & Psychotherapy
Janet Tolan

Skills in Cognitive-Behavioural Counselling & Psychotherapy
Frank Wills

Skills *in*
RATIONAL EMOTIVE
BEHAVIOUR

Counselling & Psychotherapy

Windy Dryden

Los Angeles | London | New Delhi
Singapore | Washington DC

First published 2009

SAGE Publications Ltd
1 Oliver's Yard
55 City Road
London EC1Y 1SP

SAGE Publications Inc.
2455 Teller Road
Thousand Oaks, California 91320

SAGE Publications India Pvt Ltd
B 1/I 1 Mohan Cooperative Industrial Area
Mathura Road
New Delhi 110 044

SAGE Publications Asia-Pacific Pte Ltd
33 Pekin Street #02-01
Far East Square
Singapore 048763

Library of Congress Control Number: 2008938956

British Library Cataloguing in Publication data

A catalogue record for this book is available from the British Library

ISBN 978-1-84860-669-2
ISBN 978-1-84860-670-8 (pbk)

Typeset by C&M Digitals (P) Ltd, Chennai, India
Printed in India at Replika Press Pvt. Ltd
Printed on paper from sustainable resources

DEDICATION

I dedicate this book to Francesca Inskipp, the editor of this series. Francesca has been a stalwart in the world of counselling and psychotherapy in the UK for may years and has been particularly instrumental in bringing the issue of skills to the centre stage of clinical practise, training and supervision.

CONTENTS

INTRODUCTION

The series in which this book is placed has as its theme the skills of practising different approaches to counselling and psychotherapy. In this particular volume I will focus on the skills involved in practising Rational Emotive Behaviour Therapy (REBT) effectively. In doing so, I have decided to place the skills that I am going to discuss within the context of the working alliance between REBT therapist and client. I have decided to take this particular tack for two reasons. First and foremost, I firmly believe that the good practice of any therapeutic approach is marked by the establishment and maintenance of a good working alliance between the therapist and her* client. It is also marked by a suitably good ending. Second, critics of REBT and of other approaches within the CBT tradition argue that these approaches are overly technical and neglect the therapeutic relationship. While there are, of course, technical features of REBT, its skilful practice is carried out within a good working alliance and I have structured this book accordingly (see also Gilbert & Leahy, 2007).

In Chapters 1 and 2, I begin by outlining REBT's distinctive features within the realms of theory and practice. Grasping something of the theory and practice of REBT will help you to understand the skills that I am going to discuss and exemplify in Chapters 4–7. In Chapter 3, I discuss a four-part model of the working alliance that I will be using to frame the skills considered in the rest of the book. So Chapters 1, 2 and 3 provide the necessary frameworks to understand REBT skills within the specific context of this approach's core concepts and within the broader context of the working alliance.

When I exemplify the skills discussed in Chapters 4–7, I want to make clear that I will not use actual case material since I wish to protect client confidentiality. What I will do instead is use a case example similar to the clients found in the case-load of any REBT therapist and in doing so I will use constructed dialogues that are also very typical of therapist–client exchanges in REBT. When discussing the case I will do so in the context of each chapter's focus. Thus, the presentation of case material may not always be in temporal order. Please bear this in mind as you follow the case from chapter to chapter.

While I will contextualise the skills in the manner outlined above, I want to make it clear that this book does not seek to be comprehensive in its coverage of REBT skills, particularly the many skills that can be best placed in the task domain of the working alliance. Such a book would require far more space than I have at my disposal within the structure of the series. Nevertheless, this is the first book on REBT to place the working alliance at centre stage in the practice of this therapeutic approach. As such, I think it is a valuable contribution to the REBT literature and to the present series.

Before I begin, let me say something about REBT by way of an introduction. Rational Emotive Behaviour Therapy (henceforth called REBT in this book) was the first approach to be founded in what is now called the Cognitive-Behaviour Therapy (CBT) tradition. The origins of REBT go back to the mid-1950s and thus the approach has not long ago celebrated its fiftieth birthday. Initially, the founder of REBT, Dr Albert Ellis (1913–2007), received much criticism from a field that in those days was dominated by psychodynamic and client-centred practitioners, but he persisted in promulgating his ideas and, together with Aaron T. Beck, the founder of Cognitive Therapy (see Wills, 2008), Ellis (1962) helped to establish the CBT tradition. Ironically, as I write, CBT is again under severe critical attack from non-CBT practitioners in Britain because the National Institute for Clinical Excellence (NICE) is recommending the use of CBT in the National Health Service owing to its evidence base and are not recommending the use of many other therapeutic approaches because, according to NICE, these approaches lack a similar evidence base. So 50 years later, CBT is still under attack but this time from an ascendant position (i.e. in being recommended as an empirically-supported treatment by a national body responsible for making such decisions).

The CBT tradition has now matured to the point that several approaches have emerged within this tradition. While these approaches have much in common, they all have their distinctive features. So in Chapters 1 and 2, I will outline the distinctive features of REBT (Dryden, 2008) so that you can see how it differs not only from other non-CBT approaches in this series (Joyce & Sills, 2001; Lister-Ford, 2002; Tolan, 2003) but also from the other CBT approach that appears in the 'Skills' series (Wills, 2008).

*In this book, in the main case example, the therapist will be female and the client male. This was decided on the toss of a coin.

Windy Dryden
London & Eastbourne
October 2008

1

THE DISTINCTIVE THEORETICAL FEATURES OF RATIONAL EMOTIVE BEHAVIOUR THERAPY

In this chapter, I will briefly outline the distinctive theoretical features of REBT, while in the following chapter, I will discuss the distinctive practical features of this approach. Taken together these opening chapters are a précis of a book-length work on the subject (Dryden, 2008).

Postmodern Relativism

REBT theory espouses postmodern relativism which is antithetical to rigid and extreme views and holds that, as we far we currently know, there is no absolute way of determining reality. This philosophy stops short at saying that there is absolutely no absolute way of determining reality for to do so would violate the central position of postmodernism. Thus, while REBT puts forward certain criteria to differentiate irrational beliefs from rational beliefs, it holds that these criteria are relative rather than absolute and would be against any such absolute criteria (Dryden, 2008).

REBT's Position on Human Nature

REBT theory has a unique position on human nature (see Figure 1.1 and Table 1.1). This viewpoint was put forward by Daniel Ziegler (2000) who helped to pioneer a 'basic assumptions' approach in personality theory (Hjelle & Ziegler, 1992).

	STRONG	MODERATE	SLIGHT	MID-RANGE	SLIGHT	MODERATE	STRONG	
FREEDOM		■						DETERMINISM
RATIONALITY				■				IRRATIONALITY
HOLISM		■						ELEMENTALISM
CONSTITUTIONALISM	■							ENVIRONMENTALISM
CHANGEABILITY	■	■						UNCHANGEABILITY
SUBJECTIVITY	■							OBJECTIVITY
PROACTIVITY	■							REACTIVITY
HOMEOSTASIS				■				HETEROSTASIS
KNOWABILITY						■		UNKNOWABILITY

FIGURE 1.1 *REBT's position on the nine basic assumptions concerning human nature (the shaded areas indicate the degree to which REBT favours one of the two human bipolar extremes)*

Reprinted with permission from Ziegler, D. (2000). Basic assumptions concerning human nature underlying rational emotive behaviour therapy (REBT) personality theory. Journal of Rational-Emotive and Cognitive-Behaviour Therapy, 18, 67–85. Reprinted with permission from Springer US.

Table 1.1   Description of the nine basic assumptions concerning human nature (from Hjelle & Ziegler, 1992)

Freedom – Determinism
How much internal freedom do people have and how much are they determined by external and internal (e.g. biological) factors?

Rationality – Irrationality
To what extent are people primarily rational, directing themselves through reason or to what extent are they guided by irrational factors?

Holism – Elementalism
To what extent are people best comprehended as a whole or to what extent by being broken down into their constituent parts?

Constitutionalism – Environmentalism
To what extent are people the result of constitutional factors and to what extent are they products of environmental influences?

Changeability – Unchangeablity
To what extent are people capable of fundamental change over time?

Subjectivity – Objectivity
To what extent are people influenced by subjective factors and to what extent by external, objective factors?

Proactivity – Reactivity
To what extent do people generate their behaviour internally (proactivity) and to what extent do they respond to external stimuli (reactivity)?

Homeostasis – Heterostasis
To what extent are humans motivated primarily to reduce tensions and maintain an inner homeostasis and to what extent are they motivated to actualise themselves?

Knowability – Unknowability
To what extent is human nature fully knowable?

REBT's Distinctive ABC Model

While an ABC model for understanding psychological problems can be found in different CBT approaches, REBT uses a distinctive ABC model in this respect (see Chapter 7 for examples). In this model the person is deemed to disturb herself at 'C' about a key aspect of the situation that she is in (at 'A') largely because she holds a set of irrational beliefs at 'B' (Dryden & Branch, 2008). For example:

A = My friend criticised me unfairly
B = She must not criticise me unfairly
C = Hurt

This model has a number of distinctive features:

1   It holds that 'A' is often inferential in nature.
2   As shown above, it argues that beliefs (rational and irrational) at 'B' are the central determining factor of functional and dysfunctional response at 'C' about adversities at 'A'.
3   It argues that 'C' can be behavioural and cognitive as well as emotive.
4   It also stresses that ABCs are best understood within a situational context.

Rigid Beliefs are at the Very Core of Psychological Disturbance

Perhaps the central tenet of REBT theory is that rigid beliefs are at the very core of psychological disturbance. Ellis (1994) argued that while irrational beliefs can be rigid or extreme, of the two it is rigid beliefs that are at the very core of disturbance. Rigid beliefs are often based on what may be regarded as partial preferences, but are then transformed into absolutes. Thus, if I believe that it is important to me that you like me, then this is my partial preference. When I make this belief rigid,I transform it into a demand, thus: 'I want you to like me and therefore you must do so'. It is important to note that rigid beliefs are often expressed without the partial preference being made explicit. Thus: 'You must like me'.

Flexible Beliefs are at the Very Core of Psychological Health

The corollary of the previous point is that flexible beliefs are at the very core of psychological health. Ellis (1994) argued that while rational beliefs can be flexible or non-extreme, of the two it is flexible beliefs that are at the very core of psychological health. Flexible beliefs, like rigid beliefs, are often based on what are partial preferences, but they are flexible because the person is explicit that they are not rigid. Thus, if I believe that it is important to me that you like me, then this is again my partial preference. When I make this belief flexible, I negate the demand, thus: 'I want you to like me, but you don't have to do so'.

Extreme Beliefs are Derived from Rigid Beliefs

REBT theory argues that extreme beliefs are derived from rigid beliefs (Ellis, 1994). Since the theory posits that rigid beliefs are at the very core of disturbance it follows that other unhealthy beliefs and distorted cognitions are derived from this rigid core. Extreme belief derivatives are the closest derivatives to this core. REBT theory argues that there are three extreme belief derivatives from rigid beliefs. In the material that follows I will list and define each extreme belief and show that it is derived from the person's rigid belief. These extreme beliefs are known as:

1   *Awfulising beliefs.* Here you believe at the time that something is so bad that it couldn't get any worse. For example: 'You must like me and it would be absolutely awful if you don't.'
2   *Low frustration tolerance (LFT) beliefs.* Here you believe that you cannot tolerate the adversity that you are facing or about to face. For example: 'You must like me and I couldn't bear it if you don't.'
3   *Depreciation beliefs.* Here you give yourself, others or life a global negative evaluation which, at the time, you think defines you, others or life. For example, 'You must like me and if you don't, I'm not worthy.'

Non-extreme Beliefs are Derived from Flexible Beliefs

REBT theory also argues that non-extreme beliefs are derived from flexible beliefs (Ellis, 1994). Since the theory posits that flexible beliefs are at the very core of psychological health, it follows that other healthy beliefs and realistic cognitions are derived from this flexible core. Non-extreme belief derivatives are the closest derivatives to this core. REBT theory argues that there are three non-extreme belief derivatives from flexible beliefs. In the material that follows I will list and define each non-extreme belief and show that it is derived from the person's flexible belief. These non-extreme beliefs are known as:

1   *Non-awfulising beliefs.* Here you believe at the time that something is bad, but not the end of the world. For example: 'I want you to like me, but you don't have to do so. It's bad that you don't, but not awful.'
2   *High frustration tolerance (HFT) beliefs.* Here you believe that it is difficult tolerating the adversity that you are facing or about to face, but you can tolerate it and it is worth it for you to do so. For example: 'I want you to like me, but you don't have to do so. It would be difficult for me to tolerate you not liking me, but I can tolerate it and it's worth doing so.'
3   *Acceptance beliefs.* Here you acknowledge that you, others or life are far too complex to merit a global negative evaluation which defines you, others or life. For example, 'I want you to like me, but you don't have to do so. I am the same fallible person whether you like me or not.'

REBT's Position on Negative Emotions

REBT theory distinguishes between unhealthy (dysfunctional) negative emotions (UNEs) and healthy (functional) negative emotions (HNEs). It argues that UNEs and HNEs are qualitatively different from one another as UNEs stem from irrational beliefs and HNEs stem from rational beliefs (see Dryden, 2009a). As such they exist on two separate continua rather than on one single continuum.

For example, anxiety about a threat is underpinned by an irrational belief, and its healthy alternative about that same threat is concern, which is underpinned by a rational belief. The goal in REBT is not to reduce the intensity of anxiety; rather, it is to help the person to feel concerned rather than anxious about a threat.

REBT's Explanation of How Clients Create Highly Distorted Inferences

When clients discuss their problems with their REBT therapists, it sometimes occurs that they report highly distorted inferences. Given the available evidence, it is usually easily apparent to the therapist that such inferences are negatively biased and highly skewed to the negative. However, these inferences seem very real to clients. Examples of such inferences are: 'I am going to have a heart attack', 'Nobody will ever talk to me again' and 'I will always fail and will end up a bag lady'.

REBT theory argues that such inferences are cognitive consequences (at 'C') of irrational beliefs. Such inferences are highly distorted because prior related and usually less distorted inferences at 'A' have been processed by the person using his or her irrational beliefs at 'B'. Thus:

A = I am feeling out of control
B = I must gain control immediately
C (cognitive) = If I don't I will have a heart attack

A = My friends are not talking to me
B = My friends must talk to me and it is terrible that they are not
C (cognitive) = Nobody will ever talk to me again

A = I may fail a crucial forthcoming exam
B = I must pass this exam and it will be the end of the world if I do not
C (cognitive) = If I fail, I will always fail and will end up a bag lady

REBT's Position on Human Worth

REBT theory has a unique position on human worth. Actually, it has two positions on this subject, a preferred position and a back-up position. It holds that unchangeable aspects of humans are our:

- Humanness (we are human till we die)
- Complexity (we are too complex to justify a single defining global rating)
- Uniqueness (there will never be another you)
- Fallibility (we have an incurable error making tendency).

REBT's preferred position on human worth is that we are neither worthwhile nor worthless; rather, we just are and we can either choose to accept ourselves as human and as having the above unchangeable aspects or choose not to do so. When we do make this affirmative choice we can be said to be operationalising a philosophy of unconditional self-acceptance (USA) which encapsulates REBT's preferred position on human worth.

When clients do not resonate with this position and prefer to regard themselves as having worth, then the best way of doing this without making themselves vulnerable to ego disturbance (see below) is to opt for unconditional self-worth. This back-up position states that I am worthwhile because I am human, complex, unique and fallible. I could, of course, state that I am worthless because I have these aspects, and this is equally valid for I can neither prove that I am worthwhile nor worthless. However, if I want to live healthily and happily, then the unconditional self-worth position will facilitate this far more than the unconditional worthlessness position.

According to REBT, the real culprit (apart from unconditional worthlessness) when it comes to ego disturbance is conditional self-worth. Thus, when I say that I am worthwhile when I am loved, successful, popular and wealthy, for example, then I disturb myself when I lose any of these factors and I am vulnerable to self-disturbance when I have these factors because I can always lose them (see Appendix 2).

REBT Distinguishes between Ego and Discomfort Disturbance and Health

REBT theory argues that we have two major domains in which we function as humans: ego and non-ego (here referred to as discomfort). It therefore distinguishes between ego disturbance and discomfort disturbance on the one hand, and ego health and discomfort health on the other.

Ego Disturbance and Health

Ego disturbance in the face of adversity is marked by a rigid belief and a self-depreciation belief that is derived from it. For example: 'I must pass my exam and I am a failure if I don't'. By contrast, ego health in the face of the same adversity is marked by a flexible belief and an unconditional self-acceptance belief that is derived from it. For example: 'I would like to pass my exam, but I don't have to do so. If I don't, I'm not a failure. I am an unrateable human being who has failed in this respect.'

Discomfort Disturbance and Health

Discomfort disturbance in the face of adversity is marked by a rigid belief and an awfulising belief and/or a low frustration tolerance (LFT) belief that is derived from it. For example: 'I must have the benefits that I will get if I pass my exam and I couldn't bear to be deprived of these benefits should I fail.' By contrast, discomfort ego health in the face of the same adversity is marked by a flexible belief and a non-awfulising belief and/or a high frustration tolerance (HFT) belief that is derived from it. For example: 'I would like to have the benefits that I will get if I pass my exam, but I do not need these benefits. If I fail the exam and am thus deprived of these benefits, then it would be a struggle for me to tolerate this deprivation. But I could tolerate it and it is worth it to me to do so.'

There are two other important points worth noting about these two forms of disturbance. First, a rigid belief on its own does not make clear the type of disturbance a person is experiencing. The extreme belief derivative helps to make this clear. Thus, if my rigid belief is: 'I must retain my autonomy', this belief on its own does not indicate ego or discomfort disturbance. However, if my major extreme belief derivative is: '... and I am a pathetic person if I lose my autonomy', then I am experiencing ego disturbance, whereas if it is: '...and I can't bear the resultant conditions if I lose of my autonomy', then I am experiencing discomfort disturbance.

The second important point is that ego disturbance and discomfort disturbance frequently interact. Thus, I may begin by experiencing ego disturbance and create a disturbed negative emotion such as shame, and then I may focus on the pain of this emotion and tell myself that I can't bear this emotional pain (discomfort disturbance).

Focus on Meta-disturbance

REBT recognises that once a person disturbs herself, it often happens that she disturbs herself about this original disturbance. This is known as meta-disturbance (literally disturbance about disturbance) and I gave an example of this at the end of the previous section. So, REBT has a decided focus on meta-disturbance. It also distinguishes between different types of meta-disturbance. Thus, it argues that a person can disturb herself about:

1   *Her disturbed emotions at 'C'.* A person may disturb herself either because of the pain of the emotional experience (e.g. I can't stand the pain of feeling depressed) or because of the meaning the disturbed emotion has for the person (e.g. feeling depressed is a weakness and proves that I am a weak person).
2   *Her dysfunctional behaviour or action tendencies.* Here the person focuses on what she did or what she felt like doing but did not do, and disturbs herself about one or the other, largely because of the meaning the behaviour or action tendency has for the person (e.g. I felt like punching her lights out, which is really nasty and proves that I am a nasty person).
3   *Her distorted cognitions at 'C'.* Here, a person may focus on a distorted cognition, which becomes her new 'A', and disturbs herself about the meaning that such a thought has for her. Thus, suppose the person disturbs himself about finding a young girl attractive and thinks that he may abuse her (his distorted cognitive consequence at 'C'). He may then disturb himself about this thought because he infers that is shameful and that he is a disgusting person for having it.

Biological Basis of Human Irrationality

Most approaches to CBT are based on social learning principles whereby it is held that people learn to disturb themselves. REBT also argues that human disturbance is partly learned, but it is unique among the CBT approaches in claiming that the biological basis of human irrationality and related disturbance is often more influential than its social learning basis. Thus, in a seminal paper, Ellis (1976) put forward a number of arguments in favour of the 'biological hypothesis', as it is known in REBT circles. Here are a few of Ellis's arguments:

1. People easily transform their strong preferences into rigid demands and have a difficult time giving up these demands and remain with their strong flexible preferences.
2. People are rarely taught to procrastinate and live self-undisciplined lives, but millions do.
3. People easily fall back into self-defeating patterns after they have made progress in dealing constructively with these patterns.
4. People can easily give people sound advice in dealing with their problems, but find it difficult to apply this advice consistently to themselves when they experience the same problems.

REBT Advocates Choice-based Constructivism and a 'Going against the Grain' View of Change

REBT favours what might be called choice-based constructivism in that it argues that humans have choices when constructing demands (e.g. 'You must like me') or non-dogmatic preferences (e.g. 'I want you to like me, but you don't have to do so'). Both are usually based on partial preferences and although a person may have a biologically-based tendency to construct a demand when her partial preference is strong, she does not have to do this and can choose to construct a non-dogmatic preference instead. The extent to which she does this in a meaningful way depends on the extent to which she 'goes against the grain' and thinks and acts according to the less powerful non-dogmatic preference and refrains from thinking and acting according to her more powerful demand.

REBT's Position on Good Mental Health

REBT has a clear position on what constitutes good mental health with flexibility and non-extremeness at its heart. Here is a partial list of such criteria, which is self-explanatory:

■ Personal responsibility
■ Flexibility and anti-extremism
■ Scientific thinking and non-utopian in outlook
■ Enlightened self-interest
■ Social interest
■ Self-direction
■ High tolerance of uncertainty
■ Strong commitment to meaningful pursuits
■ Calculated risk-taking
■ Long-range hedonism.

In the following chapter, I will outline REBT's distinctive practical features.

2

THE DISTINCTIVE PRACTICAL FEATURES OF RATIONAL EMOTIVE BEHAVIOUR THERAPY

In this chapter, I will consider REBT major distinctive practical features.

REBT's View on the Importance of the Therapeutic Relationship

The therapeutic relationship in REBT is deemed to be important but not curative, and draws fully on working alliance theory (Bordin, 1979) as a way of understanding the importance of bonds, views, goals and tasks in therapy. I will elaborate on this position more fully in Chapter 3.

REBT's Position on Case Formulation

REBT takes a flexible approach to case formulation using this to guide interventions, particularly in complex cases. However, it argues that one can do good therapy without making such a formulation, and holds that frequently this formulation can be developed during therapy rather than fully at its outset. However, when 'case' is deemed to be complex or a client is not making expected progress, then doing a more formal extensive case formulation may be necessary (see Dryden, 1998, for a full discussion on the REBT approach to case formulation, which is outside the scope of this volume).

REBT has a Decided Psycho-educational Emphasis

REBT has a decided psycho-educational emphasis and argues that its theory of disturbance and change as well as its core concepts can actively be taught to and learned and implemented by clients. This principle is underpinned by the idea first discussed in Chapter 1 that REBT therapists are very explicit about the REBT model and actively teach it to clients at an early stage so that they can give their informed consent before proceeding with this form of therapy. I will discuss how REBT therapists introduce the ABC model in Chapter 6 (see also Appendix 2).

REBT can be practised in a number of ways but, relevant to this topic, it is a therapy where the skills of assessing and addressing problems can be directly taught to clients so that that can learn to be their own therapist almost from the outset. Indeed, some of the material that has been devised to help clients to learn REBT self-help skills can also be used by people who wish to help themselves without formal therapy (Dryden, 2001, 2004, 2006a; Grieger & Woods, 1998). In addition, there are a number of REBT self-help books based on particular themes that also serve the same purpose (e.g. Dryden, 1999).

Skilled REBT therapists will work explicitly with clients so that together they can choose whether and when to take a skills teaching and learning approach to REBT therapy.

REBT's Preferred Treatment Order

REBT recommends a preferred order of treatment and argues that client problems should ideally be dealt with in the following order: (a) disturbance, (b) dissatisfaction, and (c) development. Disturbance is deemed to be present when the client is facing an adversity and holds a set of irrational beliefs (iBs) about the adversity. The resultant dysfunctional ways of responding (emotionally, behaviourally and cognitively) means that the client is ill-equipped to deal with the adversity while she is in a disturbed frame of mind. When she deals successfully with her disturbance she is then ready to deal with the dissatisfaction of facing the adversity since at this point the client holds a set of rational beliefs (rBs) about the adversity which has now become a focus for dissatisfaction rather than disturbance. Development issues, as the name implies, concern the client exploring ways of developing herself so that she can get the most out of her potential. She will not be able to do this as effectively as she could until she has dealt with the dissatisfaction of having an adversity in her life. Thus, her REBT therapist would encourage her to take steps to change the adversity if it can be changed or adjust constructively to the adversity if it can't be changed – while holding rational, rather than irrational beliefs – before focusing her attention on development issues.

While this is the preferred REBT order and a clear rationale will be given to and discussed with the client for using this order, if the latter is adamant that she wants to use a different order, then the therapist will be mindful of the working alliance (see Chapter 3) and encourage the client to proceed according to her preferences and review the results of doing so at a later date. There is little to be gained and much to be lost by the therapist attempting to force a client to use the preferred REBT order when she is very reluctant to do so. Indeed, an REBT therapist who does this is likely to hold rigid ideas about how REBT must be practised and is thus being irrational!

A second area where REBT has views on the order of treatment concerns whether to deal with meta-disturbance issues before disturbance issues or vice versa. The preferred order is to deal with a meta-disturbance issue first if its presence interferes with the client working on the disturbance issue in or out of the session, if it is clinically the most important issue of the two and, centrally, from a working alliance perspective, if the client sees the sense of doing so.

A final area where REBT has a preferred order of treatment is where this is suggested by a case formulation (for more information about doing an REBT-based case formulation, see Dryden, 1998).

REBT Advocates an Early Focus on Clients' Irrational Beliefs

As outlined in the theoretical section above, REBT theory hypothesises that a client's irrational beliefs (rigid and extreme beliefs) largely determine his psychological problems and, of the two, rigid beliefs are at the very core of such disturbance.

It follows from this that REBT therapists target for change their clients' irrational beliefs and particularly their rigid demands as early in therapy as is feasible. Other approaches in the CBT tradition (see Wills, 2008) argue that to focus on such underlying beliefs early on in therapy will engender resistance, but REBT therapists argue differently. They hold that as long as clients understand the role that such irrational beliefs play in determining and maintaining their problems, and appreciate that they need to examine and change these beliefs if they are to effectively address their problems, then such resistance is kept to a minimum. It is important, therefore, to realise that the skilful REBT therapist succeeds on this issue because the work that she is doing with the client is based firmly on a strong working alliance between the two (see Chapter 3).

The Importance of Constructing Rational Beliefs

Helping clients to examine and change their irrational beliefs is a key task of the REBT therapist. However, a skilful REBT therapist knows that in order to best expedite the belief change process, she first needs to help her client to construct an alternative rational belief and encourage him to understand that holding this belief will lead him to achieve his therapeutic goals.

As guided by REBT theory, if the therapist is targeting a rigid belief for change (e.g. 'You must like me'), she first needs to help the client to construct a flexible belief (e.g. 'I want you to like me, but you don't have to do so') and if she is targeting an extreme belief (i.e. an awfulising belief, an LFT belief or a depreciation belief), she first needs to help the client construct a non-extreme belief (i.e. a non-awfulising belief, an HFT belief or an acceptance belief). Thus, if the therapist is targeting an extreme, awfulising belief (e.g. 'It would be awful if you don't like me'), she would first help the client to construct an alternative non-extreme, non-awfulising belief (e.g. 'It would be bad if you don't like me, but it would not be awful'). If the therapist fails to help the client to construct a rational alternative to his irrational belief, then she will impede the change process as the client will be in a belief vacuum, being encouraged to give up his irrational belief, but without having anything with which to replace it.

While helping a client to construct a rational belief is important, the client then needs to develop and strengthen this belief if meaningful change is to occur.

REBT Recommends the Use of Logical Disputing

In keeping with other CBT approaches, REBT uses empirical questions (i.e. is the belief true or false?) and pragmatic arguments (i.e. is the belief largely helpful or largely unhelpful in disputing beliefs). Empirical arguments are designed to help the client to see that there is no empirical evidence to support his irrational beliefs, but there is such evidence to support his rational alternative beliefs.

Pragmatic arguments are designed to help the client to see that his irrational beliefs are largely self-defeating and interfere with him pursuing his healthy goals, while his rational alternative beliefs are largely self-enhancing and help him to pursue his healthy goals.

In addition, REBT advocates logical disputing of irrational beliefs. Here, the therapist helps the client to see that his irrational beliefs are illogical while his rational alternative beliefs are logical. Thus, both a rigid belief and flexible belief are based on a non-rigid partial preference (e.g. 'I want you to like me…'). When the person transforms this partial preference into a rigid belief (e.g. '…and therefore you must do so'), he creates an illogical belief because the rigid conclusion does not follow logically from the non-rigid, partial preference. On the other hand, the person's alternative flexible belief does follow because it is comprised of two non-rigid elements (e.g. 'I want you to like me … but you don't have to do so').

While REBT advocates such logical disputing, it is an open question concerning how persuasive and therefore effective such disputing is. It may be that logical disputing has more of an effect when used with empirical and pragmatic disputing and that on its own its effect is limited. Such questions can only be answered empirically.

REBT Advocates the Use of a Variety of Therapeutic Styles

While REBT advocates therapists taking an active-directive stance in therapy, particularly at its outset (see Chapter 4), it is not prescriptive about how its therapists implement that stance in terms of therapeutic style. Thus, it is possible for REBT therapists to be informal or formal, humorous or serious, self-disclosing or non-self-disclosing, Socratic or didactic, and using metaphors, parables and stories or refraining from their use. Skilful REBT therapists vary their therapeutic style according to the client they are working with, and the stage of therapy that they have reached (see Chapter 4).

REBT Discourages the Use of Gradualism

There are basically three ways of tackling emotional problems. To face problems fully, to take steps to face them in a way that is challenging, but not overwhelming (Dryden, 1985), or to go gradually. REBT discourages clients from going gradually, if at all possible, because doing so tends to reinforce their philosophy of low frustration tolerance, e.g. 'I must avoid feeling uncomfortable as I tackle my problems' (Ellis, 1983). In my experience, clients will only face their problems head on if they have powerful motivation to do so. Most clients can be encouraged to take the 'challenging, but not overwhelming' route. However, it is better to allow clients to go gradually than to threaten the working alliance. They can always be encouraged to challenge their LFT ideas and 'speed up' later.

REBT's Realistic View of Psychological Change

REBT has a realistic view of psychological change and encourages clients to accept that change is hard work and, consequently, it urges therapists to be forceful, energetic and persistent as long as doing so does not threaten the therapeutic alliance (Dryden & Neenan, 2004a). It also encourages clients to understand and implement the REBT change process as follows:

1   Understand that your problems are underpinned by irrational beliefs.
2   Set goals.
3   Construct rational alternatives to these beliefs and see that they will help you to achieve your goals.
4   Examine both your irrational beliefs and their rational alternatives and see that the former are false, illogical and unhelpful and the latter are true, logical and helpful.
5   Commit yourself to developing and strengthening your rational beliefs.
6   Act in ways that are consistent with your rational beliefs while rehearsing them and continue to do this until you truly believe them.
7   Identify and deal with obstacles to change.
8   Implement relapse prevention procedures.
9   Generalise change to other relevant situations.
10   Accept yourself for backsliding and continue to use REBT change techniques.

REBT Recommends Teaching General Rational Philosophies to Clients Whenever Feasible

While REBT therapists will as a matter of course encourage their clients to acquire, develop and maintain specific rational belief, they will also, whenever possible, offer to teach them general rational philosophies and encourage them to make a 'profound philosophic change' (changing general iBs, such as 'I must be liked by significant people', to general rBs such as 'I want to be liked by significant people, but they don't have to like me') if they are capable of doing so and interested in doing so. Not all clients will be so capable and/or interested, but if therapists do not offer to do this they may be depriving a significant minority of their clients of getting the most out of REBT.

Compromises in REBT

REBT therapists have a preferred strategy and, as we have seen, this involves encouraging clients to achieve belief change. However, it recognises that clients may not be able or willing to change their irrational beliefs, and in such cases it recommends making compromises with the ideal of belief change (Dryden, 1987). Thus, when the client is not able or willing change his irrational beliefs, the REBT practitioner can help him to:

- Change his distorted inferences
- Change his behaviour
- Learn new skills
- Change or leave the situation which provides the context for his problem.

Dealing with Clients' Doubts, Reservations and Objections to REBT

Like other therapists, REBT practitioners address client obstacles to change. However, since REBT therapists endeavour to teach salient REBT concepts, it often transpires that such obstacles are rooted in clients' doubts, reservations or objections to these concepts. It frequently transpires that these doubts etc. are based on client misconceptions of these concepts. If the REBT therapist does not elicit clients' doubts, etc., then these clients will still have these doubts and be influenced by them and they will thus resist making changes. However, as the therapist has not elicited her clients' doubts, then she will not know why the client is resisting change.

Emphasis on Therapeutic Efficiency

All therapeutic approaches are (or should be) concerned with matters of therapeutic effectiveness. REBT is also concerned with the principle of therapeutic efficiency – bringing about changing in the briefest time possible (Ellis, 1980). This is why Ellis counsels REBT therapists to adopt an early focus on clients' irrational beliefs (see p. 14) and to encourage their clients to tackle their problems full on, if possible. Ellis's concern with therapeutic efficiency had its roots in his early experiences of carrying out lengthy diagnostic procedures with clients who dropped out before the treatment phase began, which he regarded as a waste of a clinician's time and thus therapeutically inefficient (Ellis, 1962).

REBT is an Eclectic Therapy

Although REBT is clearly placed in the tradition of CBT, it can also be regarded as an eclectic therapy. Indeed, I have called REBT a form of theoretically-consistent eclecticism - advocating the broad use of techniques, from wherever, but to achieve goals in keeping with REBT theory (Dryden, 1986). However, it sometimes will use techniques that are not in keeping with REBT theory when theoretically-consistent techniques bear no therapeutic fruit (see Ellis, 2002). Ultimately, REBT therapists' primary concern is to help their clients rather than to practise REBT!

In the following chapter, I will discuss the idea that the practice of REBT is best viewed within the context of a good working alliance between therapist and client.

3

THE WORKING ALLIANCE IN REBT

Skilful REBT is practised within the context of a good working alliance between therapist and client. My own practice in this respect is very much influenced by the work of Ed Bordin (1979), who argued that the working alliance can be broken down into three such components: bonds, goals and tasks. I recently argued that a fourth component – 'views' – should be incorporated into an expanded version of Bordin's model (Dryden, 2006b), and it is this expanded model that I will present here (see Figure 3.1).

Bonds

In this section, I will consider the following issues in the bond domain of the working alliance, and in doing so, I will integrate working alliance theory with the REBT standpoint:

1   The 'core conditions'.
2   The client's feelings of safety and trust in the counsellor.
3   The therapist's stance.
4   The REBT therapist's style of doing therapy.
5   The influence base of the therapist.

The 'Core Conditions'

Whenever therapeutic bonds are considered, the pioneering work of Carl Rogers (1957) on what are known as the 'core conditions' immediately comes to mind. These concern the interpersonal attitudes of the counsellor and her impact on the client. This work has shown that when the counsellor (a) demonstrates an empathic understanding of the client's concerns, (b) is genuine in the therapeutic encounter, and (c) shows unconditional acceptance of the client as a person, and, most importantly, when the client experiences these 'core conditions', then the client tends to move to a position of healthy psychological functioning. Rogers' (1957) original position was that such experienced counsellor attitudes are necessary and sufficient for client development. This means that such conditions have to be present and that no other conditions are needed for such development to

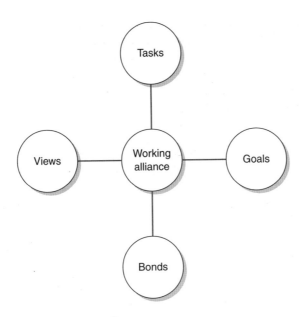

FIGURE 3.1   *The working alliance diagram*

occur. The REBT position is quite different and reflects its more flexible stance (Ellis, 1959). This position is that the presence of such conditions are often desirable, but neither necessary nor sufficient for client progress to occur. These conditions are important in REBT, not for their own sake but because they set the stage for the strategic and technical work that is to follow. My own view is in keeping with this, but also reflects the working alliance position, which is that these counsellor attitudes are often important for most but not all clients. Here the task of the REBT therapist is to emphasise and de-emphasise certain attitudes with different clients in order to establish the most productive and idiosyncratic therapeutic bond with each individual client. I will focus on the REBT approach to empathy in Chapter 4.

The Client's Feelings of Safety and Trust in the Counsellor

The second area that is relevant to our discussion of the therapeutic bond places more attention on the client's feelings and attitudes towards the counsellor. Here such concepts as the client's trust in the counsellor, feelings of safety in the relationship, and degree of faith in the counsellor as a persuasive change agent are important.

The REBT/working alliance viewpoint on this issue is as follows. The best way of helping clients to feel safe in the REBT process and at the same time communicate that one is a trustworthy person and competent practitioner is to do three things.

First, it is important that the REBT therapist establish what I have called elsewhere the 'reflection process' (Dryden, 1989). This involves encouraging the client to stand back at important junctures in order to reflect on what has been going on in that relationship. This ensures that the client knows that she has a 'voice' in the counselling relationship and both participants know that they can access the reflection process at any time to discuss any matter.

Second, the REBT therapist tends to be explicit about salient aspects of REBT theory and practice. This helps the client to know what is happening in the counselling process and thus to feel safe in the therapeutic relationship, especially because she knows that she has a voice in that relationship.

Finally, the REBT therapist takes the principle of informed consent very seriously. Thus, she is not only explicit about explaining REBT concepts and what her therapeutic plans and strategies are (i.e. the informed part of informed consent), but she also seeks to gain her client's consent to proceed (i.e. the consent part of informed consent). I discuss the skills involved in operationalising informed consent in REBT in Chapter 5.

Therapeutic Stance

The third area relevant to the therapeutic bond concerns the therapeutic stance of the counsellor. From an REBT perspective, the therapist is encouraged to adopt an active-directive therapeutic stance. Here the therapist is active in directing the client to an REBT-based assessment of his problems and to what he can do to best address this problem. In doing so, the skilful REBT therapist makes clear that this is but one perspective and that there are other perspectives that can be taken on client problems and their resolution. The principle of informed consent that I discussed above helps the client fully engage with the active-directive therapist or seek more acceptable help elsewhere.

Working alliance theory advances the point that not all clients respond well to an active-directive therapeutic stance and the skilful REBT therapist is able to vary her stance to best help her clients. In particular, she is careful to monitor the impact of her active-directive stance on clients. Thus, with clients who are particularly sensitive to what they experience as encroachments on their sense of autonomy, the REBT therapist would take care to emphasise client choice in their interactions. With clients who are particularly passive and dependent, the therapist would adopt a stance which encouraged activity and direction in the client rather than emphasise this stance herself. While it is difficult to conceive of practising REBT in a non-directive stance, skilful REBT therapists do vary the extent of their activity and directiveness according to different clients and the phase that they are at in counselling process. Typically, REBT therapists will be less active and directive during the latter stages of the process as clients take more responsibility for implementing REBT strategies themselves as they work towards becoming their own therapists. I will discuss this issue more in Chapter 4.

Therapeutic Style

It is possible to practice a particular therapeutic stance in different therapeutic styles. One therapeutic style that is relevant to the practice of REBT concerns the degree of formality of the therapist. From my experience, most of the REBT therapists of my acquaintance tend to be more informal than formal in therapeutic style. However, there is nothing in REBT theory or practice to discourage therapists from practising REBT more formally. Working alliance theory recommends that REBT therapists vary their degree of formality to accommodate their clients' preferences on this point.

The Therapist's Influence Base

A different way of looking at the counsellor–client interactive bond emerged from social psychology over 25 years ago (e.g. Dorn, 1984). Here the focus is on clients' influence preferences. The idea that counselling is an influence process is anathema to many in the field, yet it can be viewed as such given that one person (the counsellor) is trying to influence the other person (the client) to live a psychologically healthier and more resourceful life. In REBT, such influence that is exerted is done within an ethical context with the safeguards that I discussed above (use of the reflection process, explicit communication about therapeutic matters and operationalising the principle of informed consent).

The founder of REBT, Albert Ellis, conducted therapy very much from the influence base of the expert and, indeed, many people are willing to be influenced by those whose expertise they value. It does not matter to these people that they like the therapist as long as they are impressed by their expertise. However, others are more likely to be influenced by people they like. For these people, the expert status of the therapist is not important.

Again, working alliance theory recommends that REBT therapists vary the base of their influence attempts to accommodate clients' influence preferences.

One of Rogers' core conditions is therapist genuineness. I have argued from working alliance theory that therapists should vary their bond with their clients according to a number of variables which I discussed above. However, it is important that therapists vary their bond in a genuine way. Arnold Lazarus (1981) calls the therapist who does this an 'authentic chameleon'. This means that if an indicated variation in the therapist's contribution to the bond is beyond the therapist's repertoire, then the therapist should be true to herself and not attempt to make such a non-genuine variation in her behaviour.

Views

The second component of the expanded model of the therapeutic alliance is called 'views' (Dryden, 2006b). These concern the views held by the therapist and client on such relevant issues as:

The Nature of Clients' Psychological Problems

Here the REBT position is that clients' problems are determined largely by their underlying irrational beliefs.

How Clients' Problems Can Best Be Addressed

Here the REBT position is that clients' problems are best tackled by examining and changing their underlying beliefs.

The Practical Aspects of Counselling

For example, how long should counselling last, how often should sessions occur, what are the fees to be paid and what is the cancellation policy?

Clients have Views about Counselling Too

Clients are likely to come to counselling with some idea of what determines their problems and the nature of the help that their counsellor will be providing them. If we consider the latter issue, for example, these ideas may be well informed and accurate, as in the case of a person who has read about REBT, has sought a practitioner of that approach because he has resonated with it, and has a clear idea of what to expect.

However, most of the time, the client will have little idea that the REBT therapist practises REBT and may have ideas about the determinants of their problems and how these can be best addressed that may be at variance with REBT. In addition, the two may differ on their views of the practical issues mentioned above. In which case an explicit dialogue needs to take place before the client can give informed consent to proceed (see Chapter 5).

Effective Counselling Occurs when the Client's Views are Similar to the Counsellor's

Working alliance theory holds that when clients' views are similar to those of their counsellor on the above issues, then counselling is more likely to be effective than when such views are different. When they are different, these differences need to be acknowledged and openly discussed by referring them to the reflection process.

Goals

The third component of the working alliance – goals – pertains to the objectives that both client and counsellor have for coming together in the alliance. Goals are therefore the *raison d'être* of the counselling process. At first, the issue of goals in REBT appears straightforward: the client is in some kind of psychological distress, wants relief from this distress and wishes to live a more fulfilling life. The counsellor's goal is to help the client achieve his or her goals. However, the situation is often more complex than this and there are a number of issues that need to be borne in mind when goals become centre stage for consideration in REBT.

Issues with Respect to Goals in REBT

The following are important issues with respect to goals in the working alliance.

Clients May Express Goals in Vague Terms

Here, the REBT therapist's task is to help clients to specify goals in a form that makes the goals achievable.

Clients May Want to Feel Good or Neutral about Life's Adversities

The REBT therapist needs to discuss this issue and offer the more realistic position that it is healthy to have bad feelings (but not disturbed feelings) about these adversities as a prelude to dealing with them if they can be changed, or to adjust constructively to them if they can't be changed.

Clients May Want to Pursue Personal Development Goals when They are Disturbed

The task of the REBT therapist is to help them to see that if they deal constructively with their disturbance first, then they will be more successful at pursuing their development goals than if they tried to bypass their disturbance.

Clients May Express Goals that are Out of Their Control

If a client says: 'I want my mother to change' or 'My goal is to have the local council find me better accommodation', the client is stating a goal outside his control. Whenever a client says that his goal for counselling is for something or somebody to change, then this is a goal that the REBT therapist is advised not to accept as this is outside his control. In REBT it is important to renegotiate goals so that their achievement falls within the client's power (e.g. what is the client going to do differently to encourage his mother to change? What is the client going to do to persuade the council to find him better accommodation?).

Clients May Express Goals that are Based on Their Disturbed Feelings, Attitudes or Behaviour

When an anorexic client states that her goal for therapy is to lose more weight, then this is a good example of a goal based on disturbance. Here, it is important to deal with the level of disturbance first before setting concrete goals. It is for this reason that some REBT counsellors prefer not to set goals too early in the counselling process.

Clients' Goals Change during the Counselling Process

Because clients' goals for change are dynamic rather than static, counsellors need to update themselves on the current status of their clients' goals during the reflection process. (Some counsellors do this formally in specific review sessions.)

Goals and the Working Alliance

Bordin's (1979) major point about goals, and one with which REBT therapists would concur, is that good therapeutic outcome is facilitated when the counsellor and client agree what the client's goals are, and agree to work towards the fulfilment of these goals. Thus, Bordin is concerned basically with outcome goals, i.e. goals which are set as a criterion for the success, potential success or failure of the counselling encounter at its end. While there are other goals, it should not be forgotten that outcome goals are the most important and I will discuss this issue more fully in Chapter 6.

Tasks

The final component in this four component model of the working alliance pertains to tasks – activities carried out by both counsellor and client which are goal-directed in nature. REBT has its technical side and I will discuss some of its main techniques and how to skilfully implement them in some of the later chapters.

However, an alliance perspective on tasks facilitates the execution of these tasks (by both the therapist and client) because it raises the following issues.

Issues Related to Tasks

The following are important issues with respect to tasks in the working alliance.

Client Understanding of His Tasks in REBT

Does the client understand the nature of the therapeutic tasks that he is being called upon to execute in REBT? If the client does not either explicitly or implicitly understand (a) that he has tasks to perform in the REBT counselling process and (b) what these tasks are, then a potential obstacle to the client's progress through the REBT process appears. As with other potential obstacles, this may be dealt with by referring the matter for discussion to that part of the counselling dialogue that I call the reflection process, where counsellor and client step back and discuss what has gone on between them during counselling sessions. Aware of how important it is for clients to understand their role in the counselling process and, more specifically, what their tasks are in that process, some counsellors formally attempt to initiate clients into their role at the outset.

Client Understanding of the Instrumental Value of His Tasks in REBT

If the client understands the nature of the tasks that he is called upon to execute, does he see the instrumental value of carrying out these tasks? As noted earlier, tasks are best conceptualised as ways of achieving therapeutic goals. Thus, a client may understand what his tasks are but may be uncertain how carrying these out may help him to achieve his outcome goals. For example, a client may not see how disputing his irrational beliefs about competence will necessarily help him to overcome his examination anxiety. Thus, from an alliance perspective it is very important that clients be helped to understand the link between carrying out their counselling tasks and achieving their outcome goals. This holds true whether the clients' tasks are to be performed within the counselling session or between counselling sessions in their everyday lives.

Client Ability to Execute Tasks in REBT

Does the client have the ability to carry out the therapeutic tasks required of him in REBT? The question of ability is important since although the execution of particular tasks may facilitate client change, if the client is unable to carry out these, then this poses a threat to the alliance. In this case, an REBT therapist would deliberately train the client in the requisite skills.

Client Confidence to Execute His Tasks in REBT

Does the client have the confidence to execute the task? A similar point can be made here as has been made above. Certain client tasks (and in particular those that clients are asked to execute between sessions – the so-called 'homework assignments') require a certain degree of task confidence on the part of the client if he is to execute it successfully. So the client may understand the nature of the task, see its therapeutic relevance, have the ability to carry it out, but may not do so because he predicts that he doesn't have the confidence to do it. Here the counsellor is called upon to help prepare the client in one of two ways. First, the counsellor may need to help the client to practise the task in controlled conditions (usually within the counselling session) to the extent that he feels confident to do it on his own. Second, the counsellor may encourage the client to carry out the task unconfidently, pointing out that confidence comes from the result of undertaking an activity (i.e. from practice) and is rarely experienced before the activity is first attempted. Counsellors who use analogies within the experience of the client (e.g. learning to drive a car) often succeed at helping the client understand this important point.

The Therapeutic Potency of Tasks in REBT

Does the task have sufficient therapeutic potency to facilitate goal achievement? Cognitive restructuring techniques in REBT are best seen as setting the stage for later action based on belief change. On their own these cognitive techniques have limited potency (Emmelkamp et al., 1978). Thus, it is likely that the most potent tasks in REBT are those that are behavioural in nature, albeit based on rational beliefs.

Client Understanding of the REBT Therapist's Tasks

Does the client understand the nature of the counsellor's tasks and how these relate to his own? So far I have focused on issues which deal with clients' tasks. However, in addition to the foregoing, it is important that the client understands (either at an explicit or implicit level) the counsellor's interventions and their rationale. In particular, the more the client can understand how his tasks relate to the tasks of his counsellor, the more each can concentrate on effective task execution, the purpose of which, as has been stressed above, is to facilitate the attainment of the client's goals. Should the client be puzzled concerning the counsellor's tasks and how these relate to his own, he will be sidetracked from performing his own tasks and begin to question what the counsellor is doing and perhaps even the counsellor's competence. These doubts, if not explored and dealt with in the reflection process, constitute a threat at all levels of the therapeutic alliance. An additional strategy that may prevent the development of client's doubts is for the counsellor to explain, at an appropriate stage in the counselling process, her tasks and why she is intervening in the way she has chosen to do. The explicit nature of REBT lends itself to such explicit communication.

Counsellor Skill

For a long time the issue of counsellors' skill in executing their tasks in the therapeutic process has received little attention in the counselling literature. However, investigations (e.g. Luborsky et al., 1985) have brought to light an important and quite obvious point that the skill with which counsellors perform their own tasks in therapy has a positive influence on client outcome. From an alliance perspective, the degree to which clients make progress may be due in some measure to the skill with which counsellors perform their tasks. This means that we must not assume that even well trained counsellors demonstrate equal skill in performing their tasks. A further implication is that skill factors need more prominent attention in counsellor training and supervision than has hitherto been the case. Trainers and supervisors require concrete and detailed evidence concerning how skilfully counsellors have executed their tasks and need to rely less upon counsellors' descriptions of what they did in counselling sessions and more on specific ways of appraising skill (e.g. through digital voice recordings of counselling sessions or at the very least through very detailed process notes).

The emphasis on skill in this book, and in the series in which it is placed, is testament to the importance of being able to practise one's approach as skilfully as one can. In the following chapters, I will discuss how REBT therapists can improve their own skill level. I will do so, as I discussed in the Introduction, by placing relevant skills in the most appropriate domain of the working alliance. In doing so, I do not wish to create the impression that these domains are separate within the alliance. In reality, each domain interacts with every other, but this complexity is difficult to capture within the context of a book whose readership may include some who are new to REBT. So, although I have located core skills within a particular domain, please bear in mind the dynamic and interactive nature of the four domains. Having made this important point, I begin my skills-based analysis by considering core REBT skills within the bond domain of the alliance.

4

REBT SKILLS IN THE BOND DOMAIN
OF THE WORKING ALLIANCE

In this chapter, I will discuss and exemplify core REBT skills that can best be located in the bond domain in the working alliance (Bordin, 1979; Dryden, 2006b). First, I will show how the skilful REBT therapist develops a sense of teamwork in the alliance. Second, I will consider key skills associated with the core conditions of empathy, respect and genuineness made famous by Rogers (1957). Finally, I will discuss skills associated with different therapeutic stances and styles within the practice of REBT.

Teamwork Skills in REBT

Before outlining the skills used by the REBT therapist to create a teamwork approach, let me consider the nature of the team in REBT. This team is made up of the therapist, who is an expert on the REBT view of psychological disturbance and how best to address this from an REBT perspective, and the client, who is an expert on his experience. Thus, the collaboration between the two does need to take into account this reality. If both bring their respective expertise to the relationship, this facilitates the creation of an effective team. If one or both expect the other to have expertise that they do not have, then problems might arise (e.g. the client expects the therapist to know what is wrong with him based on minimal disclosure).

There are two ways in which the therapist can create a sense of teamwork. Establishing with the client an agenda for each therapy session and establishing a channel of communication that I call the 'reflection process'. There is a third way of doing this – establishing with the client a list of his problems and goals – but this is best placed in the chapter on goals (see Chapter 6) and I will discuss it there.

Establishing a Session Agenda

Although establishing a session agenda is not a routine part of REBT practice, I think it is an important way of developing a sense of teamwork and a way of using session time efficiently (see p. 17). Using session agendas originated in the pioneering work of Beck et al. (1979) on the cognitive therapy of depression. I trained at the Center for Cognitive Therapy in 1981 and was influenced by important elements of this approach, including session agendas. As elsewhere, a key skill in REBT is in providing the client with a rationale for using session agendas. This is usually done at the outset of therapy.

Providing a Rationale for the Use of Session Agendas

In this segment the REBT therapist provides the client with a rationale for the use of session agendas.

Therapist: It's useful to use our time together as productively as we can so I am going to suggest that we make an agenda of what we both want to cover in the session at the beginning of the session. What do you think of that idea?

[Note that the therapist asks for her client's opinion here, thus promoting the idea of teamwork.]

Edwin: It sounds reasonable. What would we put on the agenda?

Therapist: Well, I would want to know briefly how your week has been, and then I would want to check on any agreed assignments you have done in the preceding week. I would want to focus most of our time on the problem that you nominate to work on. What would you like to put on such an agenda?

Edwin: I'm not sure.

Therapist: No problem, but I will be asking you that each week.

Edwin: Sounds fair enough.

Therapist: I would like to close each session by devoting some time to negotiating an assignment that arose out of the work we did in the session so you can keep the therapeutic momentum going between sessions. How does that sound?

Edwin: I expected as much. Presumably I get a say in the assignment?

Therapist: Of course! This therapy is based on teamwork, so it's definitely a process of negotiation. Do you have any reservations about developing a session agenda?

[Asking for reservations is an important part of developing teamwork, among other things. Also, by doing so, the therapist is showing that she welcomes client honesty.]

Edwin: No, it seems to be a good way to proceed.

Dealing with Client Reservations about Developing a Session Agenda

If an REBT therapist responds effectively to a client's reservations about developing a session agenda (and all other matters to do with therapy come to that), such a response will help develop a teamwork attitude and shows that the therapist respects the client. Let's see how Edwin's therapist would have responded to his reservations.

Therapist:	Do you have any reservations about developing a session agenda?
Edwin:	Well it seems quite restricting?
Therapist:	In what way?
Edwin:	Well, I can see the point of structure, but sometimes I may want to talk about my concerns in a more open-ended exploratory way. There doesn't seem a place for that in the agenda.
Therapist:	Well, the cornerstone of REBT is flexibility so if there are occasions when you want to talk in a more open-ended way, then we can put that on the agenda and then we can evaluate how helpful such exploration is. How does that sound?
Edwin:	That sounds good.

By responding as she does, the therapist shows that she takes her client's concerns seriously. However, note that she also preserves the structure of the agenda by suggesting that open-ended exploration can be incorporated into REBT. Note also that the therapist suggests that they can evaluate the helpfulness of such open-ended exploration so that the client can see for himself if this departure from more standard REBT is helpful or not. If it is, it can be incorporated, as requested by the client.

An Example of Setting an Agenda

Let's now see how an REBT therapist sets an agenda with her client.

Therapist:	OK, Edwin, let's set our agenda. I'd like to put on it how your week has been and what you did for homework. What would you like to add?
Edwin:	I want to discuss the possibility of having a joint session with my wife and the main thing I want to discuss is a recurrence of my jealousy problem.
Therapist:	OK, so let's do that and then discuss a suitable assignment at the end of the session.
Edwin:	OK, but I think we can skip the week's update as I really want to focus on the jealousy episode.
Therapist:	That's fine. So, I have the following:

- Your homework from last week
- A possible joint session with your wife
- The jealousy episode and
- An assignment arising out of our discussion

	Is that the best order for you?
Edwin:	I think the joint session issue will become clearer when we have discussed the jealousy episode.
Therapist:	Fine, so let's start with your homework from last week.

Note how the therapist and her client work together to set the agenda, including deciding jointly on the most suitable order in dealing with agenda items. Now there is an inherently logical order to some recurring items. Thus, checking last session's homework assignment will generally go before the main item to be discussed since it will probably influence what is discussed. Of course discussion of this main item will almost always precede the negotiation of a homework assignment since this will be based on this discussion. However, there will be exceptions to this order, as when a client comes in very distressed and needs to focus straight away on the source of his distress. Other items can be slotted in as they make most sense to therapist and client acting conjointly.

Establishing and Maintaining the Reflection Process

Another important way of developing a teamwork attitude and approach in REBT is for the therapist to suggest to the client that they establish and sustain a channel of communication that I refer to as the 'reflection process' (Dryden, 1989). When either the therapist or her client refers an issue for discussion to the reflection process, they stand back from what they are doing and with as much objectivity as they can muster they discuss the item thus referred. Normally, items referred to the reflection process are issues experienced by either party as problematic that warrant more objective discussion. As with agenda setting, the therapist provides a rationale for the creation of this mode of communication.

Providing a Rationale for the Development of the Reflection Process

In this next segment, the REBT therapist provides the client with a rationale for the development of the reflection process.

Therapist:	From time to time in therapy, it's useful for us both to take a step back and reflect on the work that we have been doing together. Or if either of us wants to discuss something that has gone wrong, it's useful if we can say that we want to do this. Does that make sense to you?
Edwin:	I think so. What kind of issues might we discuss?
Therapist:	Anything that is on our minds. For example, I might sense that you are annoyed about something that I have said, but which you don't mention. So, I might say to you something like: 'We need to take a step back and discuss something'. Or you may think that we are not on the same wavelength over something.
Edwin:	Sounds like a good idea.
Therapist:	Can you think of a phrase that we can both use to initiate this stepping back process?

[Note that the therapist is asking the client to think of a phrase. She introduced the idea of the reflection process – without calling it that – and therefore she wants the client to make a contribution to the process.]

Edwin:	'Let's step back for a moment' sounds good enough to me.
Therapist:	Do you have any reservations about doing this?
Edwin:	None at all. It seems like a good idea.

Dealing with Client Reservations about Using the Reflection Process

Let's see how Edwin's therapist would have responded to his reservations.

Therapist:	Do you have any reservations about stepping back and discussing an issue?
Edwin:	Well, it seems a bit contrived. If either of us has something to say to the other, why can't we just say it?
Therapist:	That's fair enough. But would you mind if I use the phrase 'Let's stand back'. I find it helps me to do just that. You don't have to use that phrase, of course?
Edwin:	That's fine.

[The therapist responds affirmatively to the client's point about finding a reflection process 'a bit contrived'. However, she would like to use a phrase that would help her to step back. This exchange shows both parties respecting one another's views.]

An Example of Using the Reflection Process

Let's now see how an REBT therapist refers an item to the reflection process. Edwin has twice agreed to do a homework assignment but on both occasions he claimed not to have the time to do the assignment.

Edwin:	I'm afraid I was just too busy to do the assignment.
Therapist:	OK, Edwin, let's step back and discuss this. OK?
Edwin:	OK.
Therapist:	So the facts are that twice now you have agreed to do an assignment that we have negotiated and the last time you were quite clear in saying that you had the time to do it, but you now say that you did not do it because you didn't have the time. I'm confused. Perhaps you can clarify matters for me.

[Notice that the therapist states the facts as they seem to her and then states her feelings of confusing and asks Edwin to clarify the issue for her.]

Edwin:	Well, I guess that doing the assignment isn't a priority for me.
Therapist:	Can you help me to understand why?
Edwin:	Well, it just seems too much for me to do.
Therapist:	I can understand that. I'm wondering why you didn't tell me that...

This example nicely shows how being factual about events that the therapist is concerned about and stating her feelings of confusion helps the client to articulate his own feelings, which he felt previously unable to disclose to the therapist. The therapist then provides the client with an opportunity to discuss the reasons for such non-disclosure. The two are back to working as a team, exploring an obstacle to client change.

'Core Conditions' Skills in REBT

As I pointed out in Chapter 3, the REBT position on the 'core conditions' put forward by Rogers (1957) is that these are often important in REBT, but rarely necessary and very rarely necessary and sufficient. I stop short of saying that they are never necessary and sufficient in REBT because that would be an extreme and therefore an irrational position. The reason that they are rarely necessary or necessary and sufficient is that in general it takes a decided focus on irrational beliefs in order for clients to effect changes in these beliefs. However important the 'core conditions' may be to the development and maintenance of a good working alliance between therapist and client, on their own they do not provide such a focus. That said, in this section, I will discuss and exemplify some of the skills shown by the REBT therapist in the realm of the core conditions.

Showing Empathy with a Rational Twist

Empathy is the process of being understood by another person from one's own frame of reference. As with all the 'core conditions', the therapeutic power of empathy lies in the client's experience of being understood by the therapist rather than in the empathic communications of the therapist. This makes a discussion of the empathy skills shown by the REBT therapist problematic in that whatever I have to say about these skills may have little impact on the experience of the client in being understood. With this caveat stated, let me proceed.

Let's suppose that the client is talking about a specific situation in which he experienced his problem. Wessler & Wessler (1980) called this 'an emotional episode'. The person-centred therapist would strive to convey to the client that she understood his experience in this emotional episode. The REBT therapist would strive to do this too, but would do so using REBT's ABC framework as a guide for her responses. Thus, the term 'experience' would be too vague a term for the REBT therapist. In breaking down the term 'experience' into its component parts, the REBT therapist sets out to do the following:

1   She endeavours to convey to the client that she understands how he felt at 'C'.
2   She endeavours to convey to the client that she understands inferences that he made at 'A'.
3   She endeavours to convey to the client that she understands the irrational beliefs that he was holding at 'B' about 'A'.
4   She endeavours to convey to the client that she understands how he acted or felt like acting at 'A'.
5   She endeavours to convey to the client that she understands the thinking consequences (at 'C') that stemmed from his irrational beliefs.

So what the REBT therapist is doing that is different from the person-centred therapist, and indeed, from therapists of other therapeutic persuasions, is to use the ABC framework to convey empathy. This means that the REBT therapist is using an external frame of reference to show the client that she understands his internal frame of reference. Note that at this point the therapist uses the ABC framework implicitly and not explicitly with the client.

An Example of Empathy with a Rational Twist

Let me give you an example with appropriate commentary:

Therapist: So, Edwin, tell me what happened when you became jealous in the week.

Edwin: Well, Linda [*Edwin's wife*] and I were at a dinner party and she was talking to Gavin, to whom I have always suspected she is attracted. Anyway, I became jealous when they started laughing and joking together.

Therapist: So you first became jealous when you saw them sharing a joke and laughing together?

Edwin: Yes, the feeling was below the surface before then, but it bubbled to the surface at that point.

Therapist: So you felt underlyingly jealous before they started laughing and joking, but you really felt these feelings at that point.

Edwin: Yes, I guess I began to feel underlyingly jealous, as you put it, as soon as I saw Gavin was at the party.

[Up to this point the therapist has conveyed her understanding of Edwin's feelings of jealousy (at 'C') as he experienced them at the party. Now she will switch and strive to understand the inferences he made at 'A'.]

Therapist: So as soon as you saw Gavin was there did you see him as a threat?

[This is an important point. Edwin has not mentioned anything to do with 'threat'. The REBT therapist has introduced the idea of threat because she knows that people who experience jealousy experience the other person as some kind of threat to their relationship. So the therapist is using the REBT theory of emotions to guide her intervention here (see Dryden, 2009a).]

Edwin: To be honest, yes, I've always had the fear that he would take Linda away from me.

Therapist: So when you were feeling jealous it was about Gavin taking your wife away from you?

Edwin: Not at that point. That came later. What I was threatened about was that she seemed to be enjoying his company more than mine.

Therapist: So you were jealous about Linda enjoying herself with Gavin more than with you rather than him taking Linda away from you. Is that right?

Edwin: Yes.

Therapist: What did you do when you really experienced your jealous feelings?

Edwin: Nothing

Therapist: Did you feel like doing anything which you suppressed?

[At this point, the therapist is trying to understand Edwin's behaviour at 'C'. Since he did not do anything, he asks about his action tendency.]

Edwin: Well, I wanted to take Linda home there and then, but I didn't. Later, I felt like asking her a lot of questions about what they were laughing and joking about, but didn't because Linda hates me doing that.

Therapist: So, when you felt jealous you really wanted to get Linda out of there, but didn't. Later you had all kinds of questions about what they were sharing, but again didn't. Because you didn't act on those impulses did you have any thoughts at that time or images or even fantasies?

(Continued)

(Continued)

[In the latter part of the above response, the therapist asked Edwin about his cognitive consequences of his irrational beliefs. Note that at this point the therapist has not yet enquired about these beliefs. Because she knows that people who experience jealousy often develop jealousy-related images and fantasies, she uses this information to inform her question.]

Edwin: Well, yes, I did. I had a thought that Gavin would take Linda away from me and I had a picture in my mind's eye of them making love together.

Therapist: When did you have this thought and this image?

Edwin: Well, I had it at the party when my jealousy was at its peak and I had it later when I suppressed the urge to question her.

Therapist: So let me sum up to see if I understand what you were going through. Your problem started as soon as you saw Gavin at the party. At that point he posed a threat to you in your mind, a threat that materialised when it seemed to you that Linda was enjoying his company more than yours. Your feelings of jealousy were kind of underlying, but really surfaced when Linda and Gavin started laughing and joking together. At that point you really wanted to take Linda home, but didn't. Instead, you had a thought that Gavin would take Linda away from you and you had a picture in your mind of them making love. When you did get home, you had that picture again and that thought when you suppressed an urge to question her. Have I understood you correctly?

Edwin: Very much so.

If the therapist had just responded to what Edwin was saying, then I would venture that Edwin would not have felt so understood. The therapist used her knowledge of the cognitive-behavioural dynamics of jealousy to inform her questioning. Her questions elicited information about his suppressed action tendencies and his images that she may not otherwise have accessed.

As a general point, skilful REBT therapists use their knowledge of the cognitive-dynamics of the major unhealthy negative emotions that clients seek help for (see Dryden, 2009a).

Finally, you will note that the therapist made no attempt to find out about Edwin's irrational beliefs. This was because she had not yet introduced Edwin to the role that irrational beliefs have in emotional problems and doing so at this point would have detracted from her main purpose – to convey her empathic understanding of his experience in this emotional episode.

Unconditional Acceptance: Therapist Respect from an REBT Perspective

The second 'core condition' that I want to discuss is therapist respect. This is better known in the REBT literature as 'unconditional acceptance'. When the therapist shows that she accepts her client unconditionally, she is showing him that she views him as a complex, unrateable, fallible human being and this attitude is held unconditionally, even when the client acts very badly.

An Example of Therapist Unconditional Acceptance in REBT

Later on in therapy, Edwin admits to his therapist that he has spread an ugly rumour about Gavin as revenge for what Edwin considers as Gavin slighting him by flirting with his wife at a wedding two weeks after the dinner party episode.

Therapist:	So what was the rumour that you spread?
Edwin:	That Gavin has contracted a venereal disease. I don't know what came over me. I was eaten up with jealousy, I just wanted to get back at Gavin. I really hate myself for what I did. You must think that I am a terrible person.

[This is a real choice point for the therapist. She can take the last client statement as a rhetorical point and respond to it as a self-belief as articulated in Edwin's last but one statement. Or she can take it as a question directed at her and warranting a direct answer. The therapist follows the latter line and we pick up the dialogue at this point.]

Therapist:	Actually I don't see you as a terrible person at all.
Edwin:	But I have done a really rotten thing.
Therapist:	Yes you have. It was very much influenced by your feelings of jealousy and anger about being slighted by Gavin, but yes I agree with you it was a rotten thing to do.
Edwin:	So that must mean you think that I'm rotten.
Therapist:	No it doesn't. It means that I see you for what you are – an ordinary fallible complex human being who has acted really badly by spreading the rumour about Gavin to be sure, but who is struggling with a really difficult emotional problem and is in emotional pain and this leads him to act really badly sometimes.
Edwin:	If only I could view myself like that.
Therapist:	Well, you can, and I propose to help you to do so if that's what you want.
Edwin:	Absolutely.

The therapist tells Edwin that she accepts him and he seems to believe her. Of course, whether a client experiences the therapist as respectful will be judged by the client over time and not just on a single incident, no matter how important it is. Nevertheless, this exchange shows that the principle of unconditional acceptance can be demonstrated by therapist and taught to the client at the same time!

Congruence and Self-disclosure

The 'core condition' of congruence is sometimes known as genuineness and sometimes as openness. What these terms have in common is the following:

- The therapist is not hiding behind a façade or role
- There is consistency between what the therapist experiences and what she discloses, verbally and non-verbally
- The therapist is prepared to be honest about his experience both inside therapy and outside therapy.

I will focus on the last point (therapist self-disclosure about an aspect of her life outside therapy) because it is easiest to put into a 'skills' framework. First, let me say that the therapist will not disclose an aspect of her experience, even though it is relevant, if she judges that doing so will impact negatively on her client. In addition, not all clients value therapist self-disclosure. Thus, if the therapist is thinking of disclosing an experience without being asked to, then it is important to check first with the client if he wants to hear it before making the disclosure.

An Example of Therapist Self-disclosure in REBT

Later on in therapy, Edwin learns suddenly that he has been made redundant from his job. Work on his jealousy problem is put on hold as Edwin is preoccupied with anxiety about his future. In the course of this work, Edwin says that he is worthless without a job and thinks that he won't work again. We pick up on their dialogue at this point.

Therapist: So you consider yourself worthless and think that you will never find a job again. Is that right?

Edwin: Yes that's about the size of it.

Therapist: Would you be interested in a similar experience that I had earlier on in my career? I think it might be helpful.

Edwin: OK

Therapist: Well, I was made redundant earlier in my career and for a time I thought that I was worthless and would never get another job. While I thought like that I felt depressed and I gave up looking for jobs. But then I stood back and realised that while being redundant is a very difficult experience to deal with, it didn't define me and therefore I wasn't worthless. Once I had convinced myself of that, it was easier for me to see that while getting a new job might take a while, there was no evidence that I would never work again. This helped me to get my act together and I started applying for jobs again. I was out of work for about six months, which was a struggle, but I persisted throughout and ended up by getting a good job.

Edwin: Can you teach me to think like that?

Therapist: I'll give it my best shot!

Edwin: OK.

[At the end of the session the therapist asked Edwin directly about the value of her self-disclosure.]

Therapist: How valuable for you, if at all, was it when I shared with you my own experience of grappling with redundancy?

Edwin: Very valuable. It showed me that you had first-hand experience of coming out on top of a very similar experience and I wanted to learn from you how I could apply to my own situation how you dealt with it.

In this example of therapist self-disclosure, the therapist did the following:

1 Asked for permission to share her experience with the client.
2 Showed the client that she first thought irrationally about a similar situation and experienced negative consequences.
3 Then showed that she changed her beliefs and experienced a positive result in doing so.
4 Asked the client for feedback on the value of her self-disclosure.

Dealing with the Client's Negative Reaction to Therapist Self-disclosure

It sometimes happens that even after the therapist has asked for permission to disclose a relevant personal experience and has followed the points listed above, the client has a negative reaction to this disclosure. Here is an example of how to respond to the client's reaction.

Therapist: How valuable for you, if at all, was it when I shared with you my own experience of grappling with redundancy?
Edwin: Actually, I didn't find it very helpful.
Therapist: Oh, I'm sorry. Can you help to explain why?
Edwin: Well, your situation was very different from mine. You were at the start of your career and had more prospects than me.
Therapist: My goal was to show you that it's possible to change your attitude.
Edwin: Can't we do that without you telling me about your life. It distracts me from my situation.
Therapist: Sure, thanks for the feedback.

[Here the therapist shows that she accepts Edwin's point about the unhelpfulness of her self-disclosure and makes a mental note to refrain from using such disclosure again.]

I present a personal example of the way that I use self-disclosure in therapy in Chapter 7 (see pp. 110–11).

Therapeutic Stance Skills in REBT

As I discussed in Chapter 3, REBT therapists adopt different stances and different styles within these stances for different purposes. In this section, I will discuss two major therapeutic stances in REBT: the active-directive stance and the coaching stance, and the skills that are associated with each of them. In doing so, I will show how the therapist explains the stance to the client, elicits his cooperation before proceeding with a stance, and deals with any client reservations about him adopting a particular stance. In doing so, I will how the REBT therapist attends to the working alliance in adopting a stance that is deemed relevant to the client at a particular point in therapy.

In Chapter 7, I will consider different styles within these stances, particularly as they pertain to examining a client's beliefs.

Active-directive Stance

REBT therapists tend to favour an active-directive stance with their clients particularly at the beginning of therapy. There are several reasons for this.

1   REBT uses a specific ABC framework to assess clients' problems. Thus, the client has to be directed to provide the relevant information that will help the therapist make an accurate assessment of these problems (see Chapter 7 for a fuller discussion of assessment skills in REBT).
2   When it comes to examining irrational and rational alternative beliefs, the therapist directs the client to consider a number of issues before asking him to commit himself to strengthening his rational belief (see Chapter 7 for a fuller discussion of belief examining skills in REBT).
3   To help the client get the most out of homework assignments, the therapist directs the client to salient information concerning negotiating and reviewing these assignments (see Chapter 7 for a fuller discussion of the skills involved in negotiating and reviewing homework assignments in REBT).
4   Whenever there is an obstacle to client change in REBT the therapist directs the client to identify the source of the obstacle (see Chapter 7 for a fuller discussion of identifying and dealing with a client's doubts, reservations or objections to salient aspects of the REBT therapeutic process).

The Relationship between an Active-directive Stance and Degree of Structure

REBT tends to be a structured approach to psychotherapy. Thus, the REBT therapist uses an ABCDE framework when working with client problems where the ABC part is used when assessing problems and the DE part (where 'D' stands for disputing beliefs and 'E' for the effects of disputing) is used to promote change.

The therapist can use this structure explicitly or implicitly with clients. When it is used explicitly, the therapist provides a rationale for its explicit use and once the client has agreed, then the ABCDE framework is explicitly referred to at relevant junctures. When an explicit structure is used with a client, then the therapist employs an active-directive stance to actively direct the client to the relevant part of the framework that they are currently focusing on. I will provide an example of this later in this chapter.

REBT therapists, in the main, prefer to work with an explicit structure since doing so enables the client to understand clearly what is happening at any part of the process and enables the client to learn more easily how to use the ABCDE framework for himself.

However, certain clients do not work well with such an explicit focus and find the overt use of the ABCDE framework too constricting and/or annoying. When this happens, the skilful REBT therapist refrains from using this framework explicitly with her client, but, and this is the important point to bear in mind, she will use this framework implicitly (i.e. in her mind) and the framework will inform her interventions. In such cases, the therapist will still adopt an active-directive stance to actively direct her client to salient aspects of the ABCDE framework, but there will be no overt reference made to this framework.

Providing the Client with a Rationale for the Therapist's Active-directive Stance

Before proceeding with an active-directive stance it is useful if the therapist provides her client with a rationale for doing so. Many clients come to counselling expecting to talk a lot and the therapist to listen and perhaps not say much. Thus, an active-directive therapist may be a culture shock for such clients. Even if the client is expecting an active-directive therapist, perhaps because he knows about REBT and has sought out an REBT practitioner, there is nothing to lose in providing a rationale since this may assure the client that he is going to get what he was hoping for. Let's see how Edwin's therapist broached this subject with him.

Therapist:	So I'm glad that you feel I understand what you were experiencing in this episode. How would you have liked to have responded in this situation?
Edwin:	Well, I would like not to have been so jealous.
Therapist:	OK, let's see if I can help you do this. In order to do so, I'd like to introduce you to a framework that will help us both understand your jealousy better. If this framework makes sense to you, I will use it and ask you a number of questions that will direct you to the relevant parts of the model. So, at this point I will take an active role and direct you to those parts. How to you feel about me doing that?
Edwin:	That's fine. Since you know the framework and I don't it makes sense if you do that.

Dealing with Client Reservations about the Therapist's Active-directive Stance

Now let's see how the therapist would have responded if Edwin expressed a reservation about his therapist adopting an active-directive stance.

Therapist:	... So, at this point I will take an active role and direct you to those parts. How to you feel about me doing that?
Edwin:	I'm not too sure about it.
Therapist:	Can you tell me why?
Edwin:	Well, it sounds as if I won't be able to say what's on my mind.
Therapist:	But while adopting an active-directive stance, I would give you space to express yourself within the model. Does that ease your mind?
Edwin:	Yes it does.
Therapist:	If you think that I am stopping you from expressing yourself, can you let me know and we can talk about it? Perhaps you can refer the issue to what I have called the reflection process.
Edwin:	That sounds very reasonable.

Here, the therapist takes time to elicit Edwin's reservation and in her response tries to assure Edwin that she will give him the space to express himself within REBT's framework. She reminds Edwin that he can refer the matter to the 'reflection process' if needs be.

It may transpire that a client may be looking for a therapy where the therapy does not adopt an active-directive role. This would lead to a discussion concerning whether the therapist can do her job using a different stance or whether the client is better served by a different therapeutic approach.

An Example of the Active-directive Stance

Before the segment that follows, the therapist has introduced Edwin to REBT's ABC model and showed him the important role that beliefs play in largely determining a client's responses in an emotional episode. In the segment, the therapist is going to use an active-directive stance to help Edwin put his experience into the ABC framework. She has already elicited some of this information while showing Edwin that she understood his experience (see pp. 33–4) and will refer back to this at various points.

Therapist: OK, let's use the ABC model to understand the factors involved in your jealousy at the dinner party. Now in the ABC framework that I have introduced you to, where do your feelings of jealousy go?

Edwin: They go under 'C'.

Therapist: Is your jealousy an emotional 'C', a behavioural 'C' or a thinking 'C'?

[This is a typical skill in REBT. The REBT therapist knows the answer to this question, but is keen to encourage the client to think for himself rather than do his thinking for him. Thus, she gives him three options to choose from. While the therapist is being active in directing her client to the question of what kind of 'C' jealousy is, note that in doing so she is encouraging him to be active in the process.]

Edwin: An emotional 'C'.

Therapist: And what was your behavioural 'C' that accompanied your jealousy?

Edwin: I'm not sure I follow you.

Therapist: When you were jealous watching your wife and Gavin laugh and joke, what did you feel like doing at that time?

Edwin: Oh, I see. I felt like taking her home with me there and then.

Therapist: And what picture did you have in your mind when you decided to stay put?

Edwin: I had a picture of them making love.

Therapist: And what thought went along with that?

Edwin: The thought that Gavin would take Linda away from me.

Therapist: What kind of 'C' is that image and that thought?

Edwin: A thinking 'C'.

Therapist: Correct. Now let's see what your 'A' was. Remember that 'A' is the aspect of the situation you felt most jealous about.

Edwin: I was jealous about Linda enjoying herself with Gavin more than with me.

Therapist: That's right. Now, was it the thought that Linda was enjoying herself more with Gavin than with you that led you to feel jealous or a belief that you held about that inference.

> Edwin: From what you said it was my rigid belief.
>
> [Remember that the therapist had taught Edwin the ABC model in general before this segment.]
>
> Therapist: Now what were you demanding that led you to feel jealous when you thought that Linda was enjoying herself more with Gavin than with you?
>
> Edwin: That Linda must enjoy my company more than Gavin's.

In this segment, the therapist plays an active role in directing Edwin to the elements of the ABC framework with respect to his feelings of jealousy at the dinner party. Because Edwin understands what she is doing and has assented to her adopting an active-directive stance, then the interaction between them is smooth and they appear to be part of a team. Note also how the therapist encourages Edwin to be active in the process.

The danger of an REBT therapist adopting an active-directive therapeutic stance is that it leads the client to be passive. As REBT is a psycho-educational approach to therapy (see Chapter 1, pp. 12–13), it holds that the client will learn more effectively when he is active in the learning process. Encouraging the client to think for himself rather than doing his thinking for him is a key aspect of helping the client to be active.

The Role of Questions in the Active-directive Therapeutic Stance

A major tool that an REBT therapist has in employing an active-directive therapeutic stance is her use of questions. Such questions can be open-ended or closed depending on the purpose behind their use. I will revisit the topic of questions in Chapter 6 when I discuss their use in the disputing process. What I want to emphasise here that it is very important that the therapist listens carefully to the client's response to judge whether or not he has answered it. A client may not answer a therapist's question for a variety of reasons, and it is important to explore these reasons. He may not understand the question, the question may lead him to think of something else which he begins to talk about, or he may find the question too threatening and thus may change the subject. Here is an example of the latter.

> Therapist: So, let's suppose for a moment that your wife was enjoying Gavin's company more than yours, why must that not happen from time to time?
>
> [Here the therapist is challenging Edwin's irrational belief and has done the appropriate ground work beforehand.]
>
> Edwin: I can be fun at dinner parties. I just wasn't in the mood that night.
>
> (Continued)

(Continued)

[Note that Edwin has not answered his therapist's question.]

Therapist: I guess you weren't, but again let's suppose that Linda did enjoy Gavin's company more than yours that night. I know you really don't like that idea, but do you have to be immune from this happening?

[The therapist briefly acknowledges Edwin's point, but asks the same question in a slightly different way.]

Edwin: I'm not sure why I wasn't in the mood that night, but I wasn't.

[Once again Edwin does not answer the question.]

Therapist: Edwin, I'd like to stand back and discuss what is going on right now. Is that OK?

Edwin: OK.

The therapist then initiates the reflection process (see pp. 30–1) and discovers that Edwin is finding the therapist's approach (where he is being asked to assume that his wife did enjoy Gavin's company more his own) too difficult to contemplate. The therapist acknowledged this and took a less threatening tack with Edwin, thus preserving the working alliance.

Coaching Stance

When the REBT therapist adopts a coaching stance with her client it is usually when the client has developed skills in using REBT for himself. Thus when he brings up new emotional episodes related to his target problem or other problems, the therapist's stance reflects this reality. Rather than treat the client as if he is new to REBT, which she would do so if she adopted an active-directive stance more associated with an earlier stage in therapy, the therapist prompts the client to use what he already knows. In the same way as the therapist's active-directive stance is right for the client who, at the outset, knows little about this approach and has to be directed to use it and then learn it, the coaching stance is right for the more REBT-experienced client. Using the right stance with the client at the right time is the hallmark of a skilful REBT therapist, who is mindful of the working alliance in using one stance or the other.

Providing a Rationale for the Use of the Coaching Stance

As with the active-directive stance, before proceeding with a coaching stance it is useful if the therapist provides her client with a rationale for doing so.

Therapist:	I think we have reached a point in therapy where you have learned enough for me to use a different stance in therapy.
Edwin:	Oh really. What stance is that then?
Therapist:	Well, for example, rather than take the lead in helping you to use the ABC framework, I suggest that you take the lead and I'll prompt you if you get stuck?
Edwin:	So you think I'm up to that?
Therapist:	I think so. Let's see shall we?
Edwin:	OK.

Dealing with Client Reservations about the Coaching Stance

Now let's see how the therapist would have responded if Edwin expressed a reservation about her adopting a coaching stance.

Therapist:	... I suggest that you take the lead and I'll prompt you if you get stuck?
Edwin:	I'm not sure I want to change the way things are going in therapy. I have gotten used to your active-directive stance and it suits me.
Therapist:	I can understand that. However, my goal is to make myself redundant and to help you to be your own therapist. Adopting a coaching stance will help me to do that.
Edwin:	Well ... I can understand your reasoning, but I'm still not sure.
Therapist:	How does this sound. Let's try things the coaching way for a while and evaluate its helpfulness to you. Then, if it isn't that helpful, I can always go back to the old stance. What do you think?
Edwin:	That's reasonable.

Here the therapist understands and is sensitive to the Edwin's reservations concerning her adopting a coaching stance. She knows that Edwin is reluctant to go with the change because he has become used to her active-directive stance so she presses the point and encourages Edwin to agree to the change on the understanding that if he doesn't find it helpful after a while she can go back to her former stance. REBT therapists employ this scientific approach because they believe that often experience is a better teacher than theory and explanation in helping clients to make such judgements. Note also that the therapist is open about the reason why she wants to adopt a coaching stance with Edwin. It is part of her longer-term plan to encourage him to become his own therapist.

An Example of the Coaching Stance

Edwin has made progress at dealing with his jealousy problem and his anxiety about being made redundant. He now has a new job and wants to discuss his anxiety about doing well in it. He has learned some of the major REBT skills and his therapist wants him to use them in discussing this problem.

Therapist:	So you wanted to bring up a new problem today.
Edwin:	I start my new job and I'm really anxious about it.
Therapist:	How do you know it's anxiety and not ordinary nervousness?
Edwin:	I can't sleep and when I do I have bad dreams about getting sacked. My hands shake and I can't concentrate on anything.
Therapist:	Sounds like anxiety. So why not take the lead and use the ABC to assess the problem.

[Right at the outset the therapist encourages Edwin to take the lead.]

Edwin:	OK, 'C' is my anxiety and associated symptoms. Now 'A' is the thing I'm most anxious about ... and that is that I will make stupid errors at work. Now my irrational belief is that I must not make these stupid errors.
Therapist:	Great. Now take the lead in examining this belief.
Edwin:	OK, I'll try. Well, this belief is not true and it's not helpful to me....
Therapist:	Why isn't it true?

[Here the therapist notes that Edwin did not explain why his irrational was not true, so she prompts him to do so.]

Edwin:	Well if there was a law of nature to say that I must not make stupid errors at work, then I wouldn't do so.
Therapist:	OK, now go with the pragmatic dispute.
Edwin:	Well, the belief that I must not make stupid errors isn't helpful to me because it leads me to be anxious, lose sleep and probably increases the chances that I will make stupid errors because the belief will impair my concentration.
Therapist:	Excellent. What's next?
Edwin:	I could use the logical dispute, but I don't find that at all helpful. So, I ... I'm not sure what's next.
Therapist:	Here's a clue ... your alternative rational belief...

[When Edwin gets stuck, rather than take over, his therapist prompts him like a good coach and gives him a clue.]

Edwin:	Oh right ... so my rational belief is ... I'd prefer not to make stupid errors, but I don't have to be immune from making them....

Hopefully, this gives you a flavour of the coaching stance. To reiterate, in adopting that stance the therapist hands the reins over to the client and prompts when appropriate, rather than taking the lead herself in using the ABCDE framework. With some clients the therapist moves from using the active-directive stance to the coaching stance as a major shift in stance across the board. However, with others she will use the active-directive stance on some issues and the coaching stance with others. Here, as elsewhere, flexibility and attending to the working alliance are, together with REBT theory itself, the REBT therapist's guiding principles.

In the next chapter, I will consider REBT skills in the 'views' domain of the working alliance.

5

REBT SKILLS IN THE VIEW DOMAIN OF THE WORKING ALLIANCE

Introduction

When Bordin (1979) wrote his seminal article on the working alliance, his model of the alliance was a tripartite one, where the three components were bonds, goals and tasks. I added a fourth component called 'views' because it occurred to me that what was missing from Bordin's original model was the therapist's and client's views on key aspects of the therapeutic process.

In this chapter I will consider the skills needed by the REBT therapist as she outlines:

1 REBT's model of psychological disturbance and the ABC framework associated with it, particularly as this helps to make sense of the client's problems.
2 An idea of what REBT is like as a therapy.
3 The likely tasks that REBT therapists and clients are called upon to carry out.
4 REBT's view of the change process.

Presenting the REBT View on Psychological Problems

From an alliance perspective, the more the therapist and client agree on their views of such matters, the stronger the working alliance will be. This is not to say that therapist and client have to hold the same views on all REBT-related issues, but if they disagree markedly on any of the above-mentioned issues, doing so does pose a significant threat to the alliance. This disagreement needs to be resolved if the client is to benefit from REBT. If not, the client should be referred on to a more suitable therapy.

Barker et al. (1990) did some research on lay people's views of psychological problems, which have implications for the working alliance. They argued that when a client's view of these problems is at variance with a therapeutic approach that he is being offered, then client resistance is more likely than if he is offered an approach that reflected his view.

I have often joked that REBT would be so much easier if a new client had a computer chip inserted in his brain where the REBT view of psychological problems could be downloaded and which wiped clean the client's pre-existing view! In the absence of this chip (and, all joking aside, this idea would be anathema to REBT therapists as they value choice and freedom of thought!), it is important that the therapist engages her client in an explicit discussion about their respective views on psychological problems. There are two main reasons for this. The first reason is an ethical one. Here, the purpose of this discussion is for the therapist to outline the REBT view of psychological problems so that the client can give or withhold informed consent to proceed. The concept of informed consent is an important ethical principle and one that is enshrined in many, if not all, 'Codes of Ethics and Practice' in the field of counselling and psychotherapy. REBT takes the principle of informed consent very seriously. It holds that a client cannot be expected to give informed consent if they haven't been informed. There is a view that has emanated from social work in the USA that a client only becomes a client when he has given informed consent to proceed with a form of help that has been outlined to him and that he actively wants to make use of. Until then he is best considered an applicant for help (Garvin & Seabury, 1997). Similarly, in REBT a person only becomes a client if he understands (a) the REBT view of psychological problems, particularly as they pertain to his concerns, and (b) how REBT intends to treat these problems.

The second reason for the REBT therapist outlining the REBT view of psychological problems with her client and engaging him in a discussion about their respective views is a pragmatic one. As Barker and his colleagues note (Barker et. al., 1990; Pistrang & Barker, 1992), the closer the therapist's and the client's views on psychological problems are, the stronger the alliance in this domain and in general. A certain amount of difference in their respective views is certainly not a problem and can be expected. However, if they hold radically different views, it may mean that REBT is not a viable treatment for that client and the therapist would serve the interests of the client better if she effected a suitable referral to a practitioner of an approach that more closely approximated the client's view.

If we accept the argument that it is important for the REBT therapist to outline the REBT view of psychological problems, then the therapist is faced with a number of questions:

1   When should she do this?
2   Should she use or the client's problem in her explication or not?
3   How much information should she provide?

Let me deal with these issues and focus on the skills involved in presenting the REBT model.

When to Present the REBT View of Psychological Problems

When he was in active practice, Paul Woods (1991), a well-known REBT therapist, evolved an approach to explaining the REBT model which was quite unique. He would outline the model in detail using charts to demonstrate his points even before the client had had an opportunity of telling Dr Woods what his problems were.

Most REBT therapists would probably not take such a radical approach, mainly because their view would be that when someone seeks help he expects to tell his therapist in the first session what his problems are. So a good time to explain the REBT model is when the client has had an opportunity to discuss his problems and experience the client's understanding of those problems (see Chapter 4). A further reason for this is that if the therapist is going to use the client's problem as content while outlining the REBT model, then she needs to know what that problem is!

Of course if the client becomes very distressed while recounting his problem(s), then it would not be good practice to inform him about the REBT model at that point. So, the therapist does need to judge when the time is ripe for explaining the model. She does not have to make this decision on her own, and putting the issue on the session agenda (see pp. 27–30) and discussing with the client when to do this in a particular session is a good teamwork-building strategy (see Chapter 4).

Finally, some REBT therapists send material to prospective clients, or to clients who have made a first appointment, which outlines the REBT view of psychological problems and how it addresses these problems. I include an example of this in Appendix 1.

Explaining the REBT Model: To Use Client Material or Not

There are two major ways of presenting the REBT model to use the client's disclosed problem as content or not to do so. The advantage of doing so is that it involves the client, who can see quite clearly the applicability of the REBT view to understanding his problem. The disadvantage is twofold. First, having disclosed his problem, the client may not be in a sufficiently objective frame of mind to get the most out of the model being applied to his problem. Second, if the client has a view of psychological problems in general, or of his problem in particular, which is at variance with the REBT view, then the client may be more resistant towards accepting the REBT view under these circumstances than if the model was presented more generally and without reference to his problem. Again, this is a decision that the REBT therapist does not have to make alone. She can involve the client in the discussion, as in the following segment.

Therapist:	I'd like to outline the REBT view of psychological problems so you can see how I will make sense of your problems, but I'm in two minds about how to do this so I'd value your opinion about the best way to proceed from your perspective. OK?
Edwin:	Fine.
Therapist:	Well, I can explain it first using an example that does not reflect your problem and we can discuss that first and then apply it to the problem that you have just told me about, or I can use the problem that you have just disclosed while explaining the model. Which approach would make better sense to you?
Edwin:	I think the one where you don't use my problem. I'm still feeling a bit raw having told you about the jealousy episode so I'd probably be able to concentrate better if the example was not my problem.

How to Explain the REBT Model of Psychological Problems

There are quite a few examples in the literature of how to explain the REBT model to clients. In his public demonstrations and in early therapy sessions, the founder of REBT, Dr Albert Ellis, used what has become known as the 'Money Model'. I have included an example of him using this model to explain the REBT model in Appendix 2. Dryden & Branch (2008) have deconstructed this model and presented other relevant approaches.

In this chapter, I will present the model with a different content to illustrate that the important aspect of teaching the model is the steps that the therapist takes, not the content of the example used. As ever, an important first step is providing a rationale for the explanation.

Therapist: At this point, Edwin, I would like to outline the view that I will be taking towards your problems. It is important that I inform you about this because I will soon ask you to give your informed consent for us to proceed and you can't give your consent if you haven't been informed. OK?

Edwin: That's fine.

[There follows a brief discussion at the end of which Edwin indicates that he would prefer the therapist to present him with a version of the REBT model that does not use his problem as content. The therapist has already discovered that Edwin likes cooking, so she uses this as content for explaining the model.]

Therapist: OK, Edwin, I want you imagine that you are cooking a meal for a couple of friends and you think that they may not enjoy all the dishes. OK?

[This represents the 'A' in the REBT model, but note that the therapist does not refer to it as such. That will occur later.]

Edwin: OK.

Therapist: Now, I want you further imagine that you hold the following belief as you focus on the possibility that they may not enjoy their meal: 'I want my guests to enjoy all their food, but it isn't necessary that they do so. It would be good if they do, but not the end of the world if they don't.' How would you feel about the possibility of them not enjoying all their food if you hold that belief?

[The therapist asks Edwin to hold a rational belief at 'B' about the 'A' that she has asked him to imagine, and then asks him how he would feel at 'C'. She is hoping that Edwin will give her a healthy negative emotion (HNE) in reply.]

Edwin: I'd be concerned.

[Edwin does indicate an HNE in his answer.]

Therapist: And what would you do if you were concerned?

[Here the therapist is hoping that Edwin will see that the concern will motivate him to do well.]

Edwin: Concentrate harder to cook well.

[He does.]

Therapist: That's right, you would. Now, once again you are cooking for your friends and thinking that they might not enjoy all their food, but this time you hold the following different belief about that possibility: 'My friends must enjoy their food. They really must and it will be the end of the world if they don't.' Now how would you feel about the possibility that they might not enjoy all their food if you hold that belief?

[Here the therapist asks Edwin to imagine holding an irrational belief about the same 'A' and asks him again how he would feel at 'C'. This time, the therapist is hoping that Edwin will give an unhealthy negative emotion (UNE) in reply.]

Edwin: I'd feel very anxious.

[Edwin does.]

Therapist: And what effect would your anxiety have on your cooking?

[Here the therapist is hoping that Edwin will see that his anxiety will interfere with his cooking.]

Edwin: It will interfere with my concentration and lead me to make silly mistakes.

[He does.]

Therapist: Correct. So this model shows that when you prefer that an adversity does not occur, but don't demand that it doesn't – what we call a rational belief in REBT – then you will feel healthily bad about that adversity and be motivated to try to prevent it from happening. However, if you believe that the adversity must not occur – what we call an irrational belief in REBT – you will experience an unhealthy bad feeling and your attempt to prevent the adversity from happening may actually help to bring it about.

[Here the therapist brings the elements of the model together and in doing so shows the differential impact of rational and irrational beliefs on feelings and behaviour. The therapist will be aware that she has taught the model accurately. However, she will not yet know if the client has learned what she has endeavoured to teach him. The only way she can discover this is to ask him to put his understanding of the model into his own words.]

Therapist: Let me see if I have been clear in teaching you the REBT model. Can you put this model into your own words?

Edwin: Well, if you hold a rational belief about an adversity you get a better set of consequences than if you hold an irrational belief about the same event.

[Edwin has shown a good grasp of the model. The therapist then invites him to join her in applying the model to his disclosed problem.]

Therapist: That's a good summary. Shall we apply this model to your jealousy problem?

Edwin: OK.

What the therapist has effectively taught Edwin is the core of the ABC model, as shown below.

A = Adversity	A = Same adversity
B = Irrational belief	B = Rational belief
C = UNE	C = HNE
Dysfunctional behaviour	Functional behaviour

The skilled REBT therapist is prepared to respond to whatever the client says in response to her questions while teaching the model. I have presented an example where the client gave the 'correct' answers. I did this to help you to focus on the therapist's skills in presenting the model. Since space considerations prevent me from dealing with how an REBT therapist responds when a client provides 'incorrect answers', I refer you to Dryden & Branch (2008) for a full discussion of such eventualities.

How Much of the Model Should a Therapist Teach?

In the example above the therapist taught Edwin the differential effect of beliefs (rational and irrational) about the same adversity on emotional and behavioural consequences. As this is the core of the REBT model of psychological problems, this will suffice for many clients. However, with a client who is more sophisticated, the therapist may incorporate a few more steps into the model. Let me demonstrate this. I will first backtrack a little so you can understand the full context of what the therapist is doing.

Therapist: ... Now, once again you are cooking for your friends and thinking that they might not enjoy all their food, but this time you hold the following different belief about that possibility: 'My friends must enjoy their food. They really must and it will be the end of the world if they don't.' Now how would you feel about the possibility that they might not enjoy all their food if you hold that belief?

Edwin: I'd feel very anxious.

Therapist: And what effect would your anxiety have on your cooking?

Edwin: It will interfere with my concentration and lead me to make silly mistakes.

Therapist: OK. Now imagine that you are still holding this irrational belief as you serve your first course and your guests really love it. How do you feel about that?

Edwin: I feel relieved, delighted even.

Therapist: Right, but remember you still believe that your guests have to like all the food, so while you are relieved and even delighted that they enjoyed the first course, one thought occurs to you and you feel anxious again. What's that thought?

Edwin: Well, they liked the first course, but they might not like the second course.

[The therapist is now helping Edwin to see that when 'A' does not occur (i.e. his friends enjoyed the first course) he is relieved, even delighted. However, his reprieve

---

is short-lived. Because he is still holding an irrational belief, he disturbs himself again because it suddenly occurs to him that his friends may not like the second course.]

Therapist:	That is exactly right, but how would you feel if you still held the rational belief about the possibility that they might not like the second course?
Edwin:	Concerned, like I did about the possibility that they might not like the first course.

[The therapist helps the client to see that his rational belief protects him against disturbing himself about his friends not liking the second course in a way that his irrational belief didn't.]

Therapist:	What this shows is that when you demand that certain things must not exist, you disturb yourself when they do exist and you are vulnerable to self-disturbance when they don't exist when you think that they might. However, when you hold a non-dogmatic preference and prefer but do not demand that certain things do not exist, you are disappointed, but not disturbed when they do exist and healthily concerned when they don't because again you realise that they might occur in the future. Now could you put that into your own words... .

What the therapist has effectively taught Edwin is shown below.

A = Adversity does not materialise	A = Realisation that the adversity may still occur
B = Irrational belief	B = Irrational belief
C = Relief, delight	C = UNE

A = Adversity does not materialise	A = Realisation that the adversity may still occur
B = Rational belief	B = Rational belief
C = Relief, delight	C = HNE

Dealing with Clients' Views of Psychological Problems that are Different from the REBT Model

A client may sometimes have a view about psychological problems that is at variance with the ABC model. The skilful REBT therapist responds to the expression of this divergent view with respect, offers reasons in favour of the REBT view and engages the client in a discussion of matters arising. In the first of two exchanges that are centred on different views of the client's expressed problem, the therapist responds to the client's view that 'A' causes 'C', and in the second the client expresses a psychodynamic view of his problem.

Dealing with the Client's A–C View

When a client advances an 'A' causes 'C' view of psychological problems, he is claiming that the adversity that he faced at 'A' (either the event itself or his inference about the event) caused his dysfunctional responses at 'C'. This contrasts with the REBT view that states that the client's irrational beliefs at 'B' about the adversity at 'A' largely determines his dysfunctional responses at 'C'. Let's see how the therapist deals with this situation.

Therapist:	So, to recap, you felt jealous when you thought your wife was enjoying Gavin's company more than yours. Is that right?
Edwin:	That's right.
Therapist:	So what do you think largely determined your jealous feelings?
Edwin:	Linda enjoying his company more than mine.

[Here Edwin clearly articulates an 'A causes C' view of his problem.]

Therapist:	Would you be interested in a different view and then we can compare the two?

[This is an important intervention. First, the therapist asks Edwin if he is interested in a different view. She doesn't proceed uninvited, as it were. Second, the therapist says that they will compare the two views, thus advancing the importance of being fair-minded and building teamwork.]

Edwin:	That's reasonable.
Therapist:	OK, but first we have to assume temporarily that you are right and your wife was enjoying Gavin's company more than yours at the dinner party. REBT says that it's possible to have three different attitudes towards that event. The first is unlikely, but I will mention it anyway. It's an indifferent belief and if you held it you would believe: 'I don't care if my wife enjoyed Gavin's company more than mine'. Obviously this is not what you believed.
Edwin:	Certainly not.
Therapist:	So, you can either hold a flexible non-dogmatic preference or a rigid demand about this situation. If you held a non-dogmatic preference, you would believe something like: 'I really don't want my wife to enjoy Gavin's company more than mine, but she doesn't have to do what I want'. If you held a rigid demand, you would believe something like: 'My wife must not enjoy Gavin's company more than mine'. Now when you felt jealous which of those two beliefs did you hold?
Edwin:	Definitely the second.
Therapist:	OK. Now let's compare your view of what largely determined your jealousy and the REBT view.
Edwin:	OK, but I already see that my view is wrong.
Therapist:	Really. How so?
Edwin:	Because I resonated with the rigid demand and recognised that that was my underlying belief. Once I saw this, I realised that even if my wife did enjoy Gavin's company more than mine at the dinner party, that situation wasn't enough to explain my feelings of jealousy.

What the therapist has done here is to encourage Edwin to assume temporarily that his 'A' was true. She then outlined the REBT view and presented the three possible beliefs that he could have held about 'A'. He is then asked to choose which belief most closely approximates his experience of jealousy in the situation in which 'A' occurred and he picks the rigid demand. The therapist then asks Edwin which view better explained his jealousy. Almost before she finished asking the question, the client replied that the REBT viewpoint explained his jealousy better.

Dealing with the Client's Psychodynamic View

When a client advances a psychodynamic view concerning what largely determines psychological problems he is claiming that past relevant experience largely determines his disturbed feelings about the adversity that he faced at 'A' (either the event itself or his inference about the event). This contrasts with the REBT view, which states that the client's present irrational beliefs at 'B' about the adversity at 'A' largely determined his dysfunctional responses at 'C'. Let's see how the therapist deals with this situation.

Therapist: So, to recap, you felt jealous when you thought your wife was enjoying Gavin's company more than yours. Is that right?

Edwin: That's right.

Therapist: So what do you think largely determined your jealous feelings?

Edwin: Having my mother favour my older brother over me when I was growing up.

[Here Edwin clearly articulates a psychodynamic view of his problem.]

Therapist: Would you be interested in a different view and then we can compare the two?

Edwin: OK.

Therapist: Well, REBT argues that your mother favouring your brother over you when you were growing up would contribute to your feelings of jealousy then and may also contribute to your current feelings of jealousy, but is not enough to largely determine these feelings. Here's why. If 100 boys at the age you were then experienced their mother favouring their brother over them, would they all have felt jealous about it then?

Edwin: I guess not ... no.

Therapist: Why not?

Edwin: Because they are all different.

Therapist: And would all of these boys feel jealous as adults if they thought their wife enjoyed the company of someone like Gavin over them at a dinner party?

Edwin: No.

Therapist: Why not?

Edwin: Again, they would all be different.

Therapist: What would account for that difference?

Edwin: I don't know.

Therapist: Well, would you like to hear REBT's view of the difference?

Edwin: Very much so.

Therapist: Well, assuming that they would all prefer their wives not to enjoy the company of someone like Gavin over them, some would keep that preference flexible by believing something like: 'I really don't want my wife to enjoy this other man's company more than mine, but she doesn't have to do what I want'. Others would transform that preference into a rigid demand, and would believe something like: 'My wife must not enjoy the other man's company more than mine'. Now if some of these people feel jealous, which of these two beliefs do you think they would hold?

(Continued)

> *(Continued)*
>
> *Edwin:* The rigid demand.
> *Therapist:* And if they hold the non-dogmatic preference, how would they feel then?
> *Edwin:* Concerned or displeased, but not jealous.
> *Therapist:* Even if all those holding the non-dogmatic preference had a mother who favoured their older brother?
> *Edwin:* Even then.
> *Therapist:* So what do you conclude from that?
> *Edwin:* That the childhood experience isn't the factor that determines feelings of jealousy the most.
> *Therapist:* And the factor that does is?
> *Edwin:* The rigid demands that those who felt jealous held about the event.
> *Therapist:* And does that also apply to you?
> *Edwin:* Yes.

What the therapist did here was to acknowledge that the experience of having had a mother who favoured Edwin's brother over him probably was a contributory factor to his feelings of jealousy at the time that this happened, and may have been a contributory factor to his current feelings of jealousy. By using the 100 people technique the therapist proved to Edwin that not all boys his age who had a mother who favoured their brother over him would have felt jealous about it then. She also helped Edwin to see that not all of them would have felt jealousy currently if they all thought that their wives were enjoying the company of another man at a dinner party more than their own company. She then invited Edwin to hear the REBT view of what accounted for the different experience of those exposed to the same childhood event. When Edwin indicated that he was interested in hearing this view, the therapist outlined the REBT position as before. While the therapist could also have shown Edwin that the reason that not all 100 boys would have felt jealous at the time when their mother favoured their brother was that they held rational beliefs at the time, she felt it sufficient to show the impact of the different beliefs in the contemporaneous setting of the dinner party. At the end of this sequence, it is clear that Edwin can see that, regardless of his childhood experience, it was his currently held irrational belief that largely accounted for his currently experienced jealousy.

Presenting the REBT View on Therapy

Once the therapist has helped the client understand the role that irrational beliefs play in psychological problems in general, and in his problems in particular, she should fairly easily be able to show him that the major goal of REBT is to help people in general, and him in particular, deal effectively with their problems by changing these beliefs. I will demonstrate how the therapist helped Edwin to see this presently.

First, though, let me relate a personal experience which sensitised me to the importance of therapist and client having similar views about therapy. Many years ago when I was living and working in Birmingham, I received a phone call to my private practice from a man who wanted to know if I practised 'RT'. While I thought that the way he phrased his request was a little strange, I did know that RET (as REBT was known at the time of the phone call) used to be known as 'Rational Therapy' or 'RT' and I thought that by 'RT' he was referring to RET's previous set of initials. The man duly attended for his appointment, told me a little about his problems and I responded empathically and gave him a brief description of RET, its view of psychological problems and its view on the practice of the therapy. He politely listened to me and when I asked him for his feedback. He said this: 'If I can be honest with you, that is a load of intellectualised claptrap. I thought you practised Reichian Therapy (which he referred to as 'RT'). Now do you know any Reichian Therapists in Birmingham because I certainly don't want the therapy that you practise!' I thanked him for his honesty and resolved to help him find a Reichian Therapy, which I duly did and he thanked me for the referral. I heard later from him that he was very much helped by his Reichian Therapist. For those of you unfamiliar with Reichian Therapy, it is based on the view that psychological problems are based on energy blockages that can be located in the body and that the practice of the therapy is focused on helping the person by releasing these blockages, often by deep massage. Is it any wonder that this man considered RE(B)T to be 'a load of intellectualised claptrap'. I saw no point in trying to advance a case for RE(B)T to this gentleman. He made it quite clear what he was looking for and it definitely wasn't RE(B)T. Indeed, if I had persisted with advancing a case for RE(B)T in such circumstances, I would have been acting like a salesman rather than a therapist, and some would have argued that I would have been acting unethically trying to persuade a client to accept a service he clearly did not want.

Lazarus (1973) conducted an interesting experiment which showed the power of a person's treatment preferences. He offered the same procedure to two groups of people. One group (let's call them Group A) had previously indicated preferring hypnosis over relaxation and the other group (Group B) had indicated preferring relaxation over hypnosis. Half of each group were told that the procedure they were getting was hypnosis and the other group were told that it was relaxation. The results showed that people who had their treatment preferences met found the procedure of more benefit than those who did not have their preferences met.

Making Use of the Client's Treatment Preferences in Explaining REBT

What Lazarus's (1973) research indicates is that it is important for the therapist to discover the client's treatment preferences (including what he is not looking for) before explaining REBT to the person. If the person has had previous experience of therapy, then the therapist is advised to discover what he found both helpful and unhelpful about that experience so that she can incorporate the helpful aspects in her explanation of REBT and show how REBT does not include those unhelpful aspects.

An Example of Explaining REBT to a Client

Before the segment that follows, the therapist helped Edwin to understand REBT's view of psychological problems and the key role that irrational beliefs played in his particular problems.

Therapist:	Edwin, when you decided to make an appointment to see me, what kind of help were you hoping to get?
Edwin:	Well, I'd had therapy before and I wanted to try a different approach.
Therapist:	Why was that?
Edwin:	Well, I have seen two therapists before. The first didn't say much which I didn't find helpful and the other one was more active and helped me to see the childhood roots of my problems, which was interesting, but didn't help me in the here and now.
Therapist:	So it sounds like the unhelpful aspects of the two therapies you have experienced were that the first therapist wasn't active and the second didn't help you in the here and now. Is that right?
Edwin:	Yes.
Therapist:	What were the helpful aspects of those therapies?
Edwin:	Well, the first therapist was unshockable and the second was quite empathic.
Therapist:	So would I be right in saying that you are looking for a therapy where the therapist is understanding and unshockable and is quite active in helping you in the here and now?
Edwin:	Yes, and who can teach me skills that I can use for myself.
Therapist:	So would you be interested in a brief overview of REBT to see if it the kind of therapy that you are looking for?
Edwin:	That would be good.
Therapist:	Well, I've already helped you to see the key role that irrational beliefs play in underpinning your problems. In REBT my main goal is to help you to learn the skills of identifying, challenging and changing these beliefs so that you can develop and strengthen healthy alternatives to these beliefs. Does that make sense?

[Note that the therapist has incorporated Edwin's stated wish to learn skills.]

Edwin:	So you are going to teach me those skills?
Therapist:	Yes, I am, and in a fairly active way too.
Edwin:	Great!
Therapist:	During this process, I certainly hope that I convey that I understand and I hope that I am unshockable. Please tell me if I seem shocked, by the way. And in REBT we generally do focus on the here and now. How does that sound?
Edwin:	It sounds like everything I have been looking for.

Note how the therapist incorporated all the helpful aspects of Edwin's previous therapy and indicated that REBT would offer him everything that he wanted from his previous therapies, but did not get.

Dealing with Client's Unrealistic Treatment Preferences

It is important, of course, that the therapist doesn't present a false picture of REBT in incorporating what the client is looking for and distancing REBT from what the client is not looking for. If the client wants something that REBT can't provide, then it is important that the therapist is clear about the fact that REBT can't provide that factor. Here is how I deal with this issue when I run REBT group therapy.

Windy: OK group, how many of you want to deal with your problems very quickly, at a moderate pace or slowly?

[The group members indicate their preferences by a show of hands.]

Windy: ... OK, I see that you all want to deal with your problems very quickly ... Now how many of you want to be very comfortable, moderately uncomfortable or very uncomfortable in addressing your problems?

[The group members again indicate their preferences with a show of hands.]

Windy: ... So you all want to be very comfortable in addressing your problems. So let's sum up. You all want to address your problems very quickly and be very comfortable doing so. Well, sadly, REBT can't do that for you since that's magic. In REBT, if you want to address your problems very quickly, unfortunately you will have to put up with being very uncomfortable doing so. And if you want to address them at a moderate pace, then you will have to tolerate being moderately uncomfortable. But if you want to be very comfortable, you will have to address your problems so slowly that it will take you ages to deal with them. So what's it to be group?

The above is usually said with a good deal of humour, but it has a serious point, and that is that in REBT the speed at which the client addresses his problems usually correlates with the degree of discomfort experienced. Albert Ellis used to tell a story of one of his clients that encapsulates this point very nicely. I often tell this story to my clients when this issue is raised.

Ellis's client was seeking help for elevator phobia, but was making very slow, if any, progress, largely because she did not want to experience any discomfort in addressing her problem. Ellis and the fellow group members (for the client was seen mainly in group therapy) had little success in dissuading the client from her freedom of discomfort approach to addressing her problem. Then late one Friday afternoon, the client requested an emergency session at Ellis's earliest convenience, so he saw her first thing on Saturday morning. It transpired that the woman, who was a secretary, worked in a large corporation whose offices were based on the second floor in a skyscraper. Late on Friday afternoon they announced that they were moving to larger offices on the 97th floor of the same building and that all workers were to report for work on the 97th floor at 9am Monday morning. This is what the woman said to Ellis:

> Woman: While I worked on the second floor I had no real need to expose myself to dis-
> comfort in dealing with this problem. It was an inconvenience having the prob-
> lem, but I could work my way round it. Now I can't. I can easily walk up two
> floors, but no way can I manage to walk up 97 floors. Dr Ellis, I love my job so
> I need to get over my problem by Monday morning. You have to help me. I'll do
> anything!
>
> Ellis: Even make yourself very uncomfortable?
>
> Woman: I will gladly put up with great discomfort if I can take the elevator to the 97th
> floor on Monday morning.
>
> Ellis: OK, well, I want you to spend the weekend going up and down all the ele-
> vators you can find in New York. The taller the building, the better.
>
> Woman: Will the World Trade Center buildings do.
>
> *[Author's note: This was well before the tragic events of 9/11.]*
>
> Ellis: Keep going up and down the elevator in the World Trade Center until you make
> yourself comfortable. Then go to the Empire State Building and do the same.
> Go to as many tall skyscrapers, including the one where you work, and keep
> going up and down those elevators until you get over your fear.

And that is exactly what she did. It was particularly windy that weekend, but
she didn't allow that to stop her even though some of the elevators were shaking
in the wind. She kept going up and down elevators all weekend, including the
building where she worked, and by Monday morning she had completely overcome
her fear of elevators.

This story nicely shows that if a client does truly want to address her problems
quickly she can make great progress if she is prepared to tolerate great discomfort.
Ellis's client was thus prepared because she had a powerful reason to do so,
which shows the value of appealing to the client's goals at relevant junctures in
the therapeutic process (see Chapter 6).

In the following segment, I show how Edwin's therapist would have addressed
an unrealistic treatment preference if he had expressed one.

> Edwin: One thing, I'm not looking for work to do between sessions. I have a lot on
> at work and don't have the time to take on any extra tasks.
>
> *[Edwin's statement poses quite a threat to the working alliance as an integral part of REBT
> is client execution of negotiated between-session assignments (see Chapter 7).]*
>
> Therapist: Now that could be a sticking point about me taking you on at this time
> because, to be frank, so-called homework assignments are an integral part
> of this therapy.
>
> Edwin: Oh, I see.
>
> Therapist: When you said that you weren't looking for work to do between sessions
> because of your current workload at work, how much time would be too
> much for you?
>
> *[Before discussing the principle of homework in REBT any further, the therapist seeks
> more information.]*

Edwin: A couple of hours a day.

[It is rare for clients to do that much daily homework and rare for therapists to expect their clients to do that much work every day. So the therapist's requests for information quickly reveals a client misconception.]

Therapist: How much time would you be prepared to devote to such work?
Edwin: About 30 minutes a day.
Therapist: I think we can work with that.
Edwin: Oh great. That's a relief.

I remember reading a story about a footballer and his agent agreeing between themselves that they would accept a salary of £20,000 a week from a club that was keen to sign the player. The club secretary (who was in charge of making financial offers to prospective players) walked in and said outright that he was sorry, but the club could offer no more than £30,000 a week for the player's services. Containing their glee, the agent and player feigned disappointment and managed to negotiate an extra £2,000 a week from the club representative! The REBT therapist was intuitively using the moral that can be taken from this story: Don't discuss the principle of homework with a client until you know how much time the client is prepared to devote to it. Here Edwin was dismissing the principle of homework because he wrongly thought that he was expected to devote two hours a day to it.

Views on Therapist and Client Tasks

Every approach to counselling and psychotherapy expects both therapist and client to contribute to the therapeutic process. In Chapter 7, I will discuss the skills that are associated with the therapist's tasks in REBT. In this section, I will consider tasks (both the therapist's and the client's) from a views perspective and discuss how the therapist can outline her tasks, and those expected of her client in REBT, so that her client knows what to expect of his therapist and knows what is expected of him as a client.

Therapist: Would it be helpful if I outline how I see my role as a therapist?
Edwin: That would be useful.
Therapist: Well, I have already said, my main role is to help you to identify, challenge and change your irrational beliefs to rational beliefs. To help you to change these beliefs I will, with your active collaboration, suggest how you can put into practice in your life what you learn in therapy sessions. Any questions so far?
Edwin: Sounds what I expect. But what about teaching me the skills?

(Continued)

(Continued)

Therapist:	That's a big part of it. I can certainly teach you the skills of REBT so you can learn to become your own therapist. Another important task that I have is to help us identify and deal with any obstacles to change that we encounter along the way. How does all that sound?
Edwin:	That's good.
Therapist:	Do you have any doubts, reservations or objections to how I see my role in therapy?
Edwin:	Not at the moment.
Therapist:	Let me know if you think of any. OK?
Edwin:	OK.
Therapist:	Now, what do you think your role is in REBT?
Edwin:	Well, to tell you what my problems are and be honest.
Therapist:	Good.
Edwin:	To learn and practise the skills you are going to teach me. That's about all. ... Oh and to carry out the assignments that we have agreed that I do between sessions. ... That's it.
Therapist:	I would just add to disclose your doubts, reservations and objections to any-thing I may say. OK?
Edwin:	That's a deal.

Presenting the REBT View on the Therapeutic Change

The final area in the views domain that I want to discuss is REBT's view on therapeutic change. This is important because if a client has an unrealistic view of therapeutic change, then this will affect his participation in the change process. One particular unrealistic view of therapeutic change is where the client thinks that intellectual insight into his irrational beliefs is sufficient for meaningful change to occur.

Two Types of Insight

In an early and classic article, Ellis (1963) made an important distinction between two types of insight in REBT. In the first, called 'intellectual insight', the client has an intellectually-based understanding that his irrational beliefs are irrational (i.e. false, illogical and largely unconstructive) and his rational beliefs are rational (i.e. true, logical and largely constructive). However, this insight has little impact on the client's feelings and behaviour.

In the second type of insight, called 'emotional insight', the client has an emotionally-based strong conviction that his irrational beliefs are irrational (again false, illogical and largely unconstructive) and his rational beliefs are rational (again true, logical and largely constructive). This insight does have an impact on the client's feelings and behaviour.

As you can see from the above, intellectual insight has, on its own, little or no impact on the client's feelings and behaviour, and therefore is of little use in the pursuit of the client's healthy goals.

You will see that distinguishing between the two types of insight plays an important part in the therapist's explanation of the change process in REBT.

When to Present the REBT View of Therapeutic Change

There are two main occasions when an REBT therapist can outline the REBT view of therapeutic change. At the beginning of therapy before informed consent is sought from the client or after the client has achieved intellectual insight on the first problem that he has presented in therapy. My own practice is to do this when the client has achieved such insight, but I will also do this with clients who prefer to understand the entire process of REBT before giving informed consent to proceed. As with other matters, the skilful REBT therapist does not make such decision unilaterally, but will share her thinking with her client and seek his view on the matter. Making a joint decision will strengthen the working alliance.

An Example of Explaining the REBT View of Therapeutic Change

Here is an example of the therapist explaining the REBT view of therapeutic change to Edwin. The therapist decides to do this after Edwin has achieved intellectual insight into his irrational beliefs, which underpin his jealousy, and into his alternative rational beliefs.

Therapist: OK, so now you can see why your irrational beliefs are irrational and why your rational beliefs are rational. In REBT this is what we call intellectual insight. Do you think that's enough for you to deal with your jealousy problems?

Edwin: I seriously doubt it.

Therapist: That's right. Do you know why?

Edwin: Not really.

Therapist: Well, it will become clear if I explain the REBT view of therapeutic change to you. Would you be interested in learning about this view?

Edwin: That would be useful.

[Note once again that the therapist asked Edwin if he was interested in the REBT view of therapeutic change before giving the explanation. Only when Edwin assented did his therapist begin her explanation. Note that the therapist uses an analogy to explain the process of therapeutic change and then applies the learning points to Edwin's situation.]

Therapist: Let me explain this by using an analogy. Do you play tennis?

Edwin: I used to when I was a boy.

(Continued)

(Continued)

Therapist: OK, good. I want you to imagine that as a boy you wanted to learn to play tennis properly, so you saved up your pocket money to pay for professional tennis lessons. On your way to your first lesson, you meet your uncle who asks
you where you are going. You tell him and he says that he plays tennis really
well and he will teach you how to play for nothing. You are thrilled because you
get to learn tennis and keep your pocket money so you readily agree. So over
the months, your uncle gives you weekly tennis lessons and you practise
everything he teaches you. Like a very diligent student, you do your homework. Unfortunately, your uncle turned out to be a Walter Mitty character and
in reality he was a poor tennis player and an even worse teacher. What he
actually taught you was how to play tennis poorly and you put a lot of time into
practising tennis that way, which you discovered when boys younger than you
beat you hands down.
Undeterred, you saved up your money again and this time you went to a tennis professional. You showed him your strokes and he showed you what you
had been doing wrong. He demonstrated how to play tennis properly. Now,
is just seeing what you have been doing wrong and how to put it right sufficient to improve your game?

Edwin: Not at all.
Therapist: Why not?
Edwin: Because I would have to practice playing the strokes correctly to improve.
Therapist: So knowing what you did wrong and knowing what to do to put it right is what
we call intellectual insight in REBT. It's not enough in tennis and it's not
enough in therapy either. Having that knowledge is important in knowing what
to do and what not to do, and that knowledge will inform your later practice,
but that's all it does. Indeed, that's all it's meant to do.
Edwin: I can see that clearly.

*[Note that the therapist has convincingly shown Edwin what intellectual insight can do
and, more importantly, what it can't do. Note also that she draws a parallel between tennis and therapy.]*

Therapist: Now you are really determined to learn how to play tennis properly. So you
practise all the correct shots that your tennis teacher has shown you. But
what do you think is going to happen when you try to play a shot correctly?
Edwin: My first instinct will be to play it in my usual wrong way.
Therapist: So what will you need to do at that point?
Edwin: I will need to correct myself.
Therapist: And will that feel comfortable or uncomfortable?
Edwin: Definitely uncomfortable.
Therapist: And what will it take for you to be comfortable playing the stroke correctly?
Edwin: A lot of practice.
Therapist: That's right and that's the same with changing your irrational beliefs to
rational beliefs. Your first instinct will be to think irrationally, but you can
correct that. It will feel uncomfortable to do so and it will also feel uncomfortable to act in ways that are consistent with your new rational belief
because you have been used to acting in ways that are consistent with your
irrational belief. Can you see that?

Edwin:	I can.
Therapist:	So what do you need to do to feel comfortable with your new rational belief?
Edwin:	Put in a lot of practice in thinking rationally and acting in ways that are consistent with that rational belief until I believe it.
Therapist:	That's quite right. Now can you put into your own words the REBT view of change. I'll help you if you get stuck.

[Note how the therapist draws parallels between the change process in tennis and therapeutic change, particularly emphasising the importance of practice at thinking rationally and acting in ways that are consistent with that rational belief. After helping Edwin to put the REBT view of therapeutic change into his own words, the therapist encourages Edwin to voice any doubts about this view, but he has none.]

When to Seek Informed Consent from Clients in REBT

There are three major reasons for the therapist explaining REBT's views about the various aspects of REBT theory and therapy that I have discussed in this chapter:

1   To strengthen the working alliance between therapist and client.
2   To help the client understand key ideas and therefore get the most out of REBT.
3   To enable the client to give informed consent to proceed.

Let me close this chapter by considering the question of how much information should clients be given before they can be said to have given their informed consent to proceed. As I mentioned above, some clients, albeit a minority, want to understand all the aspects that I have covered in this chapter before they will give their informed consent to proceed. Such clients tend to be careful individuals who won't commit themselves before they have all the facts at their disposal. It is important that therapists respect the position of such clients and not pathologise it, provide the relevant information and, if necessary, give these clients time to mull the issue over for a time.

My own view is that the minimum amount of information that a client needs to be given in order to be said to have given informed consent to proceed is the REBT view of psychological problems and of therapy.

In the next chapter, I will consider REBT skills in the goals domain of the working alliance.

6

REBT SKILLS IN THE GOAL DOMAIN OF THE WORKING ALLIANCE

Introduction

Like other social encounters, psychotherapy is a purposive activity. Its main purpose is to help one of the parties (the client) achieve something. The other party also achieves something from the encounter (e.g. financial reward, satisfaction, a sense of meaning and purpose), but this is not the main reason why the two are meeting. As I say, the purpose is for the client to achieve something from their meetings.

At first, it may seem obvious what the client wants to achieve from therapy. He is in pain and seeks relief from that pain. However, a closer look at the issue of goals in psychotherapy reveals a hidden complexity. In this chapter, I will attempt to address some of this complexity. It surrounds the issue of goals within the working alliance.

A discussion of the client's goals is only meaningful when viewed within the context of his problems, and I will begin my discussion of goals in REBT with showing how the therapist helps the client develop a list of problems and goals that are informed by REBT theory.

Helping the Client Develop a List of Problems and Goals

In Chapter 4, I discussed the use of session agendas in REBT agenda. I pointed out that I had taken this idea from my cognitive therapy colleagues. Another idea that I have borrowed from cognitive therapy is that of helping a client develop a list of the problems that they wish to address in therapy (Beck et al., 1979) and a corresponding list of goals with respect to these problems. What I have to do is to help clients to put these problems and goals into a framework informed by REBT theory so that they can get the most out of REBT (Dryden, 2001).

Putting a Client's Problems into the REBT Framework

In order to help the client put their problems into the REBT framework, the REBT therapist elicits the following from the client:

1   The context in which the problem typically occurs, if relevant.
2   The main inferential theme at 'A' about which the client disturbs himself.
3   The client's unhealthy negative emotion (UNE) at 'C'.
4   The client's dysfunctional behaviour or action tendency at 'C'.
5   The client's grossly distorted subsequent thinking at 'C', if relevant (see Chapter 1, p. 8).

Before I show how an REBT therapist can skilfully elicit this information, I will give few examples of client problems expressed in this way:

1   Whenever I have to give a talk in public [context] I get anxious [UNE at 'C'] about saying something foolish ['A'] so I over-prepare my material and drink alcohol before the talk to calm myself [behavioural 'C'].
2   Whenever one of my friends has something that I don't have, but want ['A'], I feel unhealthily envious [UNE at 'C'] and I can only think about this object and how to get it [thinking 'C'] and I will do anything to get it [behavioural 'C'].
3   Whenever people are late for a meeting with me [context], I get unhealthily angry [UNE at 'C'] about their lack of respect for me ['A']. I only wait for them for a minute [behavioural 'C'] but think about how I can get my revenge on them [thinking 'C'].

An Example of Putting a Client Problem into the REBT Framework

In the following segment the therapist is helping Edwin put his jealousy problem into the above REBT framework. We will assume that the therapist has not asked Edwin for a specific example of this problem and thus does not know about the episode where Edwin felt jealous when thinking that his wife was enjoying Gavin's company more than his own at the dinner party.

Therapist: So when you typically experience jealousy what seems to you to be the common factors?

Edwin: Well, my jealousy is always about my wife. And it is in situations when she is interacting with an attractive man and I think she is really enjoying his company.

Therapist: Do you ever feel jealous when you know she is interacting with attractive men and you are not physically present?

[Here the therapist's question is informed by her knowledge of the dynamics of jealousy (Salovey, 1991).]

Edwin: Only when I know that a specific attractive man is going to be there whose company I think she will particularly enjoy.

Therapist: Edwin, what is threatening to you about your wife enjoying the company of these attractive men?

[It is important to note that when helping clients to formulate their problems, the REBT therapists bring to this enterprise knowledge about the cognitive-behavioural dynamics

(Continued)

(Continued)

of these problems. This knowledge enables them to skilfully help clients formulate their problems. I recommend consulting Dryden (2009a), where I provide the REBT perspective on the major unhealthy negative emotions that clients seek help for: anxiety, depression, guilt, shame, hurt, unhealthy anger, unhealthy jealousy and unhealthy envy. Appendix 3 presents a summary of this information in tabular form. At this point, the therapist is using her knowledge that the key inference at 'A' in jealousy is 'threat to my relationship' to inform her question. Let me just remind you of this question before we continue the dialogue.]

Therapist:	Edwin, what is threatening to you about your wife enjoying the company of these attractive men?
Edwin:	That she might enjoy their company more than mine.
Therapist:	And this theme is present whenever you experience jealousy?
Edwin:	Pretty much.
Therapist:	And then when you feel jealous, what do you do at that point?
Edwin:	Well, I know my wife, Linda, really doesn't like me showing that I'm jealous, so I tend to stay quiet.

[Edwin displays no overt behaviour because he knows that his wife really does not like him doing so. In such circumstances the therapist will assess for the presence of suppressed action tendencies.]

Therapist:	But what do you feel like doing when you experience jealousy about these threats, but actually don't do?
Edwin:	First, I want to take Linda right away from the guy. I mean leave wherever we are. And if I can't do that, I want to get her to stop talking to him and start talking to me.

[The therapist has now assessed Edwin's action tendencies at 'C'. She is now going to focus on his subsequent cognitive activity at 'C'.]

Therapist:	OK and when you are suppressing these urges to act, as it were, what thoughts, images and fantasies do you have?

[The therapist is again using her knowledge of the dynamics of jealousy that the thinking consequences of irrational beliefs (which are not being assessed here as it is too early to do so) often occur as images as well as thoughts.]

Edwin:	I have the thought that the guy is going to take Linda away from me and sometimes I have a picture of them having sex.

[The therapist has enough information to put Edwin's jealousy problem into the REBT framework. After some negotiation over the form of words, the therapist and Edwin agree on the following.]

'Whenever I see my wife enjoying the company of an attractive man (context), I think that she is enjoying their company more than mine (A) and I feel jealous about this (UNE at 'C'). When I feel jealous I feel like taking my wife right away from the guy or get her to talk to me rather than him (behavioural 'C'), but I do none of these things. Instead, I think that the guy is going to take my wife away from me and sometimes I picture them having sex (thinking 'C').'

Putting a Client's Goals with Respect to his Problems into the REBT Framework

In order to help the client set a goal with respect to each of his problems and put this into the REBT framework, the REBT therapist elicits the following information:

1   The context in which the problem typically occurs, if relevant.
2   The main inferential theme at 'A' about which the client disturbs himself.
3   The client's alternative healthy negative emotion (HNE) at 'C'.
4   The client's alternative functional behaviour or action tendency at 'C'.
5   The client's realistic subsequent thinking at 'C', if relevant.

Before I show how an REBT therapist can skilfully elicit this information, I will provide the client's goals for each of the problems listed on p. 65. It might be useful to refer back to the relevant material when you read each goal.

1   Whenever I have to give a talk in public [context] I want to feel concerned rather than anxious [HNE is the desired new 'C'] about saying something foolish ['A']. I want to prepare my material rather than over-prepare it, and I want to refrain from drinking alcohol before the talk to calm myself. Instead, I will have a cup of tea [new behavioural 'C'].
2   Whenever one of my friends has something that I don't have, but want ['A'], I want to feel healthily envious rather than unhealthily envious [HNE is the desired new 'C']. Instead of being completely consumed about the object and about how to get it, I want to think carefully if it is what I really want [new thinking 'C']. If it is, I will take reasonable steps to get it rather than do anything to get it. And if it isn't what I really want, I will not take any steps to get it [new behavioural 'C'].
3   Whenever people are late for a meeting with me [context], I want to feel healthily angry rather than unhealthily angry [HNE is the desired new 'C'] about their lack of respect for me ['A']. I will wait for them for 20 minutes rather than leave after a minute [new behavioural 'C'], and rather than think about how I can get my revenge on them, I will think about how to assert myself with them when they turn up [new thinking 'C'].

There are two major points that I want you to note about these goals:

1   The context and the 'A' are the same in the person's problem and goal.
2   Healthy goal-related 'Cs' are explicitly contrasted with unhealthy problem 'Cs'.

The Context and the 'A' are the Same in the Client's Problem and Goal

You will note from these goals that the contexts and inferences are the same for both the client's problem and his goal. There is a very good reason for this. REBT theory argues that the best time to modify the situation or context in which the problem occurs or to question the inference that the client has made at 'A' is when the client is in a rational frame of mind. In order for the client to be in a rational frame of mind he has to operate from a rational belief rather than an irrational belief. Framing problems and goals from an REBT perspective is a task engaged in by therapist and client normally well before the client has learned to identify, challenge and change his irrational belief in favour of his alternative rational belief. Thus, goal-setting assumes temporarily that the context described by the client is accurate and that the inference he made at 'A' is true. This needs to be discussed with the client and I will demonstrate how this can be skilfully done in the goal-setting example presented later.

Healthy Goal-related 'Cs' are Explicitly Contrasted with Unhealthy Problem 'Cs'

If you compare each formulated problem with its formulated goal, you will note that in the latter each healthy 'C' (emotional, behavioural and thinking) is contrasted with the original unhealthy 'C' (emotional, behavioural and thinking). In the goal statement you will see that the phrase 'rather than' is frequently used. In my view, it is important to include such statements so that the client keeps these contrasts in the forefront of his mind. As I will discuss in the following chapter, belief change is based on the client acting and thinking in ways that are consistent with his developing rational beliefs and refraining from acting and thinking in ways that are consistent with his irrational beliefs. Having these contrasts in his goal statement will help the client to convert his goal-related behavioural and thinking 'Cs' into actual behaviour and thinking respectively.

An Example of Putting a Client Goal into the REBT Framework

In the following segment the therapist is helping Edwin construct a goal with respect to his jealousy problem and put this goal into the REBT framework.

Therapist: So let's see what would be a realistic goal in terms of your responses when you see your wife talking to an attractive guy and you think that she enjoys his company more than she does yours.

[Here the therapist suggests that they set a goal helping him to respond constructively when he sees his wife talking to an attractive man and he thinks that she enjoys the man's company more than she does his. In REBT terminology, she is encouraging the client to assume that the context and his inference are accurate for the time being.]

Edwin: Can't you help me think that she enjoys my company more than his?

[The client indicates that he is more interested in changing his inference at 'A'.]

Therapist: That is an important thing for us to do. Do you the think that the best time to do that is when you are disturbed about your wife enjoying some other man's company more than yours or when you are in an objective frame of mind about it.

Edwin: The latter.

Therapist:	So that's why I suggest that we first help you to get into an objective frame of mind about your wife enjoying some other guy's company more than yours and then you will be in a better place to question it. Does that make sense?
Edwin:	Yes it does.
Therapist:	So I suggest that I help you set a goal to deal with this situation as healthily as you can.
Edwin:	Sounds good.

[The therapist has given Edwin a plausible rationale for constructing a goal where he handles as best he can the situation where his wife does enjoy the company of an attractive man more than his company. Edwin understands this strategy and assents to it.]

Therapist:	Instead of feeling jealous, what would be a healthy emotion that you could feel about this? It will need to be a negative feeling since your wife finding the company of another man more enjoyable than your company is a negative event, but it will also need to be healthy feeling.
Edwin:	That's a tough one.
Therapist:	OK. I will come back to that because I think it will easier for you to nominate such feeling when you have set behavioural and thinking goals.

[The therapist could have suggested a few relevant healthy negative feeling alternatives to jealousy and that would be an alternative approach when a client cannot nominate such a feeling for himself. However, she chooses an alternative strategy for, as she says, a client is more likely to nominate such a feeling when she has set behavioural and thinking goals at 'C'.]

Edwin:	OK.
Therapist:	You say that when you are jealous you suppress an urge to take Linda right away from the guy and to engage her in conversation instead. What could you do instead at this point that would be constructive?
Edwin:	I could engage someone else in conversation without frequently checking on my wife.
Therapist:	Sounds good. Would you like to set that as your behavioural goal?
Edwin:	Yes I would.
Therapist:	OK. Now instead of thinking that the guy is going to take Linda away from you and having a picture of them having sex, what realistic thoughts and pictures would it be healthy for you have?
Edwin:	That she is enjoying talking to the guy and that's all it means.
Therapist:	How about adding in all probability?
Edwin:	Why do you suggest that I add that?
Therapist:	Well, when I see my husband talking to an attractive woman I don't know for certain that they won't go off together. They probably won't and probabilities are all we have in life.
Edwin:	Sounds reasonable.
Therapist:	You sound doubtful.
Edwin:	It's just like it would be nice to have such certainty.
Therapist:	It sure would, but where are you going to get it from?

(Continued)

(Continued)

Edwin [laughing]:	OK, I get the picture!
Therapist:	So your thinking goal is?
Edwin:	That Linda is enjoying talking to the guy and that's all it means, in all probability.
Therapist:	Now let's go back to your feeling goal. What would you call the feeling that goes with this scenario? You see your wife talking to an attractive guy and think that she is enjoying his company more than yours. You want to handle the situation better, so you engage someone in conversation and refrain from checking on your wife while thinking that she is enjoying the other guy's company and that is all it means in all probability. What healthy negative feeling could you feel instead of jealousy?
Edwin:	Concern.
Therapist:	And would that be a good feeling goal for you?
Edwin:	Yes it would.

[The therapist has enough information to put Edwin's goal into the REBT framework. After some negotiation over the form of words, the therapist and Edwin once again agree on the following.]

'Whenever I see my wife enjoying the company of an attractive man (context) and I think that she is enjoying their company more than mine ('A'), I want to feel concerned about this rather than jealous (HNE is the desired new 'C'). Instead of engaging in, but not acting on the urge to take my wife right away from the guy or to get her to talk to me rather than him, I'd rather engage someone else in conversation without checking on my wife (new behavioural 'C'). I am going to work towards thinking that my wife is enjoying the guy's company and that's all it means in all probability, rather than to dwell on the idea that the guy is going to take my wife away from me and rather than picturing them having sex (new thinking 'C').'

Problems and Goals with a Specific Example of a Client's Target Problem

The REBT therapist will typically work with a client on one problem at a time. This problem is called a 'target problem' because both therapist and client are targeting that problem for change. The goal with respect to that target problem can therefore be thought of as a 'target goal'.

When the therapist and client start work on the client's target problem, the therapist will ask the client to provide a specific example of this problem. Since the client experiences his problems in specific contexts, this strategy is designed to bring therapy to life. An important part of working with a specific example of a client's target problem that is relevant to this chapter is having the client and therapist agree on their understanding of the nature of the problem, as experienced in the specific context, and the client's goal with respect to this specific example. With respect to this goal, the therapist can ask the client how he would have preferred to have dealt with this situation (i.e. past focus) or, if the situation were to happen again, how he would like to handle the situation differently (i.e. future focus).

If the therapist has done her job well in putting the client's unexemplified general problem and associated goal into the REBT problem and goal framework, then putting the specific example into this framework should be relatively straightforward. This is because the specific problem and goal should have the same or similar components as the general problem and goal that it exemplifies. If, for any reason, the REBT therapist finds herself putting a specific example of a client's problem into the REBT problem and goal framework without having done so for the general problem, she should still follow the framework as outlined earlier in this chapter (see p. 65 and p. 67).

The therapist had little difficulty putting Edwin's specific problem into the REBT problem and goal framework as the specific elements of both problem and goal were almost perfectly derived from the general problem and goal. However, for the record, I outline below the written summary that the therapist and Edwin made of the specific example of his problem and associated goal.

Edwin's specific problem

'When I saw my wife laughing and joking with Gavin at the dinner party [context], I thought that she was enjoying his company more than mine ['A'] and I felt jealous about this [UNE at 'C']. When I felt jealous, I felt like taking my wife right away from Gavin or getting her to talk to me rather than to him [behavioural 'C'], but I did neither of these things. Instead, I thought that Gavin was going to take my wife away from me and I pictured them having sex [thinking 'C'].'

Edwin's goal related to his specific problem (i.e. how he would like to respond to it if it happened again)

'When I saw my wife laughing and joking with Gavin at the dinner party [context], I thought that she was enjoying his company more than mine ['A']. I would like to feel concerned about this rather than jealous [HNE is the desired new 'C']. Instead of engaging in, but not acting on, the urge to take my wife right away from Gavin or to get her to talk to me rather than him, I'd rather engage someone else in conversation without checking on what is happening between my wife and Gavin [new behavioural 'C']. I'd rather think that my wife is enjoying the Gavin's company and that's all it means in all probability rather than dwell on the idea that Gavin is going to take my wife away from me and rather than picturing them having sex [new thinking 'C'].'

How to Respond when Clients Express Goals in Vague Terms

When clients are often asked what they want to achieve from therapy in an open-ended way and without close reference to their problems, as above, they often respond in vague terms. Thus, they may say that they want to feel happy or they may say what they don't want to feel (e.g. 'I don't want to feel anxious'). In both cases, the task of the therapist is to take their statement and work with them until they specify a realistic specific goal.

Responding to a Client Who Wants to Feel Happy

> *Therapist:*   So what would you like to achieve from therapy?
> *Client:*   I want to feel happy.
> *Therapist:*   In what ways are you not happy?
>
> *[Here the therapist is looking for the client's problems so she reverses his vague statement.]*
>
> *Client:*   Well, I'm not happy in my love life and I'm not happy in work.
> *Therapist:*   Which area shall we start with?
>
> *[Note how the therapist begins to narrow down the search for problems and from there the client's goals.]*
>
> *Client:*   Let's start with work.
> *Therapist:*   In what ways are you not happy at work?
> *Client:*   Well, I'm upset with my boss.
>
> *[The client is still being vague, but this time about his problem (I feel upset).]*
>
> *Therapist:*   What are you particularly upset with your boss about?
> *Client:*   Well, he keeps piling work on me but doesn't do that with others on the team.
> *Therapist:*   Has he tried to do this with others in the team?
> *Client:*   Yes, but they just say 'no'. So he gets me to do it.
> *Therapist:*   So you don't say 'no' then?
> *Client:*   No, I don't.
> *Therapist:*   Would you like to?
> *Client:*   Yes I would.
> *Therapist:*   And if you did say 'no' and he stopped giving you extra things to do, would you be happier at work?
> *Client:*   Definitely.
> *Therapist:*   So would one of your goals be to assert yourself with your boss and say no to him when he gives you extra work to do?
> *Client:*   That would be good.

Working quite carefully, the therapist gradually helps the client to focus on a problem at work and helps the client to state a specific goal. So the therapist has helped the client go from 'I want to be happy' to 'I want to assert myself with my boss and say "no" to him when he gives me extra work to do'.

Responding to a Client Who Doesn't Want to Feel Disturbed

Another situation where a client expresses a vague goal is when he says that he doesn't want to feel disturbed, but does not specify what he does want to feel. Since the client does not live in an emotional vacuum, particularly where he previously disturbed himself, the REBT therapist will not accept this as a goal, but will work with the client to specify the presence of a healthy goal given the nature of the adversity the client is facing. Here is an example of how to do this.

Therapist:	So what problem can I help you with?
Client:	I get anxious about approaching women I find attractive.
Therapist:	What are you anxious about with respect to approaching them?
Client:	I'm anxious that I might get rejected.
Therapist:	And what would you like me help you achieve with respect to this problem?
Client:	Well, I don't want to feel anxious.
Therapist:	So you don't want to feel anxious about the prospect of being rejected by women. How do you want to feel about this prospect.
Client:	I'm not sure. All I know is that I don't want to feel anxious.
Therapist:	I can appreciate that, but since we don't live in an emotional vacuum, I think you need to feel something.
Client:	I can see that.

[Since the therapist is not finding it easy helping her client find an appropriate healthy negative emotion, she widens her strategy and enquires about his behavioural 'C'.]

Therapist:	When you feel anxious about approaching women what do you do?
Client:	I avoid approaching them.
Therapist:	And do you want to approach them?
Client:	Definitely.
Therapist:	So we know that anxiety won't help you do that. Right?
Client:	Right.
Therapist:	And we know that you can't live in an emotional vacuum. Right?
Client:`	Right.
Therapist:	So you only have one option left. Do you know what that is?
Client:	No.
Therapist:	Would you like to know?
Client:	Of course.
Therapist:	Well, I can help you feel concerned, but not anxious about the prospect of being rejected by women. If you feel concerned but not anxious, you would still approach women. What do you think of that goal?
Client:	Concern and approaching woman rather than anxiety and not approaching them? I'll take it.

The therapist works with the client to the point where she helps him to see that he only has two options and that he wants a third option (i.e. 'to not feel anxious'), which does not exist. By linking concern with approaching women and contrasting it with anxiety and not approaching women, the therapist helps the client choose a goal. This goal is to feel concerned about the prospect of being rejected by women but approaching them anyway.

How to Respond When Clients Want to Feel Good or Neutral about Life's Adversities

Sometimes when a client is talking about an adversity and the therapist asks him about how he would like to deal with this adversity, the client replies that he either wants to feel good or to feel neutral about it. Here is how to deal with each situation.

Responding to a Client Who Wants to Feel Good in the Face of an Adversity

Therapist:	So what problem are you grappling with at the moment?
Client:	I am facing the threat of redundancy.
Therapist:	And how do you feel about this threat?
Client:	I feel very worried about this threat.
Therapist:	And how can I help you with this?
Client:	Well, I would like to feel good about my life.
Therapist:	But would you like me to help you with this threat of redundancy?
Client:	Well, I want to feel good.
Therapist:	OK, let me ask you a question. Is being made redundant a good thing, a bad thing or a neutral thing?
Client:	A bad thing.
Therapist:	So how can I help you feel good about something bad?
Client:	I guess you can't.
Therapist:	You say that at the moment you are very worried about the threat of redundancy. Is your worry healthy or unhealthy for you?
Client:	Unhealthy.
Therapist:	In what way?
Client:	Well, it doesn't help me problem-solve and it keeps me up at night.
Therapist:	So I guess I need to help you find a negative emotion since redundancy is a negative event, an emotion that will help you to problem-solve and gives you a good night's sleep.
Client:	That would be good.
Therapist:	Well, how about worry-free concern?
Client:	That sounds realistic.
Therapist:	Any doubts?
Client:	No, but I will let you know if I have any.

What the therapist did here is to show the client that it is not realistic to feel good about a negative event. Rather, it is realistic to feel negative about a negative event. Then the therapist helped the client to see that he had a choice between feeling unhealthily bad or healthily bad. By linking worry with failure to problem-solve and sleeplessness, she interested the client in a negative emotion what would help him problem-solve and not interfere with his sleep. This is what the therapist called worry-free concern. This is an interesting version of the 'I want to feel concerned rather than worried' phrase discussed earlier in the chapter. Once the client saw that concern was the healthy negative feeling alternative to worry, he accepted it as a goal.

Responding to a Client Who Wants to Feel Neutral in the Face of an Adversity

Here is an example of how to deal with a client who wants to feel neutral in the face of an adversity.

Therapist:	So how do you feel about your girlfriend ending your relationship?
Client:	I feel depressed about it.
Therapist:	And how would you like me to help you deal with her ending your relationship?
Client:	Well, I want to feel neutral about it.
Therapist:	The only way I can help you to do that is to get you to convince yourself that you don't care.
Client:	Can you do that?
Therapist:	Only if you are prepared to lie to yourself.
Client:	How do you mean?
Therapist:	Well, the truth is that you do care that your girlfriend ended your relationship. If you didn't care you wouldn't feel depressed about it. You would feel nothing and that would be the truth. But as I say, you do care. How am I going to persuade you not to care about something that you do, in reality, care about?
Client:	I guess you can't.
Therapist:	That's right.

[By showing the client that he does care about his girlfriend ending the relationship, the therapist helps the client to see that she can't help him not care about something that he does care about.]

Therapist:	What I can do is to help you feel sad, but not depressed about your girlfriend ending the relationship.
Client:	What's the difference?
Therapist:	Well, when you feel depressed what do you do?
Client:	I withdraw into myself and try to pretend I don't care when I do.
Therapist:	Well, would you like to admit to yourself that you do care about the loss of the relationship and allow yourself to mourn this loss while staying connected with others?
Client:	Well, yes.
Therapist:	Well sadness will do all that for you. So your choice is depression or sadness.
Client:	Then sadness it is.

Having disposed of feeling neutral as a viable goal, the therapist explains that the client can either feel depressed about the loss or sad about it. By contrasting the different responses associated with each emotion, it becomes clear to the client that sadness is the healthier option and the client accepts it as a feeling goal in the face of his loss.

How to Respond when Clients Want to Pursue Personal Development Goals or Address their Dissatisfaction when they are Disturbed

Clients often come to counselling with a variety of goals. Some may be related to their emotional problems, while others may seek to promote the clients' personal development, while yet others may be related to addressing areas of dissatisfaction. Especially when these are related (i.e. where the client is disturbed about being dissatisfied or wants to develop himself in the same area), REBT theory argues that it is important for the client to first address his disturbance and then work to address the dissatisfaction or develop himself in that area (see Chapter 2, p. 13). The reason for this is that if the client attempts to work on his dissatisfaction or towards his personal development goals when he is disturbed, his disturbance will interfere with the work on the other areas. So let's see how an REBT therapist responds when a client wishes (a) to work on his area of dissatisfaction rather than his disturbance, or (b) to pursue personal development goals while he is disturbed.

Responding to a Client who Wants to Address Dissatisfaction Rather than Disturbance

Therapist:	So you are revising for your exams, but when you sit them you are letting yourself down by your poor exam technique?
Client:	That's right.
Therapist:	And how do you feel when you are taking the exam?
Client:	Very anxious.
Therapist:	About what?
Client:	Mainly about going blank.
Therapist:	So to sum up, you have two problems. You are dissatisfied with your exam technique and you are anxious about going blank in the exam. Is that right?
Client:	That's correct.
Therapist:	What would you like to achieve from counselling?
Client:	I would like to improve my exam technique.

[Note that the client has expressed a goal related to his dissatisfaction about his exam technique and not related to his anxiety. The therapist will now provide a rationale for working towards a disturbance-related goal first.]

Therapist:	Do you think that the best time to do that is when you are anxious about going blank or when you are concerned, but not anxious about it?
Client:	I see what you mean. When I am concerned but not anxious.
Therapist:	So this is what I suggest. Let's first help you be concerned, but not anxious, about going blank and then we can work on improving your exam technique. Does that make sense?
Client:	Yes, that sounds sensible.

But what if the client still wanted to work towards improving his exam technique first? Here the therapist could put forward a more persuasive rationale for focusing on the disturbance first, although if she did so, she might put a strain on the working alliance. She could go along with the client's choice without any proviso or further discussion, or she could do what the therapist in the segment below did.

Therapist:	So this is what I suggest. Let's first help you be concerned, but not anxious, about going blank and then we can work on improving your exam technique. Does that make sense?
Client:	But if you help me improve my exam technique, I wouldn't be anxious.
Therapist:	OK, let me suggest this. Let's work on improving your exam technique first, but if your anxiety gets in the way, we will deal with that until it stops being an impediment. How does that sound?
Client:	Much better.

What the therapist has done here is to go along with the client's choice with the proviso that if his disturbance interferes with addressing his dissatisfaction issue, then they refocus their attention and deal with the client's anxiety. The alliance is thus preserved and a sense of teamwork strengthened.

Responding to a Client who Wants to Work Towards Personal Development Goals when he is Disturbed

Client:	Great news! I've been presented with an opportunity to join a select group at work, giving presentations to chief executives. But I have to get really good at presentations. Can you help me?
Therapist:	Well, that's not my area of expertise, but I know a colleague who specialises in this.
Client:	Oh great, what I had in mind is that we take a break and I see your colleague and once my presentations get really tip-top, we can resume. What do you think?
Therapist:	Well, I have two thoughts. First, you are a free agent and can do exactly what you want. However, I do have a reservation about that way of going about things.
Client:	What's that?
Therapist:	Well, we have just started working on addressing your anxiety about doing things wrong in presentations. Even if my colleague helps you to really become excellent at presentation skills, my concern is that your anxiety may interfere with you putting them into practice where it matters – in front of the chief executives.
Client:	But if I become really excellent at these skills, I wouldn't feel anxious, would I?
Therapist:	Well, let's see. Let's suppose you develop really excellent skills and you are just about to give your first presentation to the chief executives when you think that you might make a mistake. Given your belief, which we had just identified last session, namely: 'I must not make mistakes when I give presentations', how are you going to feel?
Client:	I see what you mean. I am going to feel anxious.
Therapist:	And what impact is your anxiety going to have on your newly acquired presentation skills?
Client:	Yes, I'm with you, it will impair them.
Therapist:	If you don't take this opportunity to join the elite group, will there be others?
Client:	I could accept, but defer it for three months.
Therapist:	Which will give us time to deal with your anxiety and then I can refer you to my colleague. How does that sound?
Client:	Great. Actually I feel relieved!

Here the therapist helped the client to understand that he could learn to develop his already good presentation skills to the point of excellence, but because he held an irrational belief about making a mistake in a presentation, his resulting anxiety would impair the execution of his newly acquired excellent skills in this area. The client accepted this point and the therapy team then refocused on helping the client work towards becoming undisturbed (but not unconcerned) about making mistakes in presentations.

If the client had been adamant that he wanted to pursue his personal development goal first, then the therapist would have adopted what might be called the 'client choice, proviso-based' approach, which I discussed and exemplified in the previous section (see p. 76).

How to Respond When Clients Express Goals that are Out of Their Direct Control

Sometimes when a client is asked for his goal in therapy, he says that he wants a change in someone or a set of conditions that are outside his direct control. In such situations there are usually three factors present:

1) The client's disturbed feelings about the conditions that currently exist.
2) The client's behaviour that could potentially influence the conditions to change.
3) The conditions themselves.

So when the client says that he wants a change in someone or a set of conditions that are outside his direct control he needs to be shown that such a goal cannot be accepted in REBT. Rather, he needs to set the following goals, preferably in this order:

1   A relevant healthy negative emotion if the client is disturbed about the conditions as they exist at present (i.e. point 1 above).
2   Behaviour that could lead to the conditions changing (point 2 above).

Here is an example of how an REBT therapist helped her client set goals that were within his control when he first expressed a goal that was not within his direct control.

Therapist:	So how can I help you?
Client:	I have a problem in my relationship with my girlfriend.
Therapist:	What's the problem?
Client:	Well basically she keeps flirting with other men when we go out.
Therapist:	And how do you feel when she does that?
Client:	Really, really angry.
Therapist:	OK, and what's your goal for coming to see me?
Client:	I want her to stop flirting with men.

[The client expresses a goal that is not within his direct control.]

Therapist:	I understand, but let me ask you a couple of questions first. OK?
Client:	OK.
Therapist:	Who governs your behaviour?
Client:	I do.
Therapist:	Can other people influence you to change?
Client:	Yes.

Therapist:	But who has the final say in you changing your behaviour?
Client:	I guess I do.
Therapist:	Is this the case with your girlfriend too?
Client:	Yes, sadly, but yes.
Therapist:	So that's why I can't accept your goal as you have expressed it because your girlfriend's flirting behaviour is within her direct control and not yours. Can you see that?
Client:	Yes, I can, but where does that leave me?

[The client can now see that his originally expressed goal is not within his direct control.]

Therapist:	Well, you said earlier that others can influence you to change your behaviour. Do you remember?
Client:	Yes.
Therapist:	Well up to now how have you tried to influence your girlfriend to stop flirting with men?
Client:	By shouting at her?
Therapist:	And has that worked?
Client:	Clearly not.
Therapist:	So I can help you come up with other ways of trying to influence her and then you can try them out and see what works. Does that seem a good way forward?
Client:	Yes it does

[The client now accepts a goal that is within his direct control, i.e. his attempts to influence his girlfriend's behaviour.]

Therapist:	You said earlier that you feel really, really angry about your girlfriend's flirting behaviour. Is that still the case?
Client:	Very much so.
Therapist:	Now do you think that your anger is the kind of anger that is going to help you or hinder you in experimenting with different influence attempts?
Client:	It will definitely hinder me.
Therapist:	So how about if I first help you to experience the kind of anger that is going to help you do this and then we start talking about and experimenting with different influence attempts. Does that order make sense?
Client:	Yes it does.

[The client now accepts the REBT preferred order: first work towards HNE goals, then work towards changing your behaviour to influence a change (in this case) in someone else's behaviour.]

How to Respond When Clients Express Goals that are Based on their Disturbance

It sometimes happens that clients' goals are influenced by their disturbance. An obvious example, as I pointed out in Chapter 3, is a client with anorexia who wants to lose more weight. However, more subtle instances of this phenomenon occur in therapy and in the following sequence I will show how an REBT therapist can skilfully respond to this issue.

Therapist:	How can I help you?
Client:	I am scared about driving and need you to help me to drive without being so anxious. Being apprehensive is OK, but the anxiety is stopping me from getting back on the road.
Therapist:	OK. You said 'get back on the road'. I'm not sure what you mean by that.
Client:	Well, I passed my driving test ages ago, but haven't wanted to drive until about a couple of weeks ago, when I discovered that I was anxious about driving.
Therapist:	I'm curious. What happened a couple of weeks ago that reawakened your desire to drive?
Client:	My sister bought a sports car and I really want one too.
Therapist:	So if she hadn't bought the sports car, would you want to drive?
Client:	Not really.
Therapist:	Let me ask you a question that might seem a bit off track. OK?
Client:	OK.
Therapist:	How do you feel about your sister having a sports car when you want one, but don't have one?
Client:	Really envious.
Therapist:	So do you think we have to help you with your anxiety about driving when it seems that you really don't want to drive, or your feelings of envy towards your sister?
Client:	My feelings of envy.
Therapist:	OK, now there are two types of envy: unhealthy envy where you only want something because someone else has it, or healthy envy where you want something for its own sake. Which type of envy do you have towards your sister and her sports car?
Client:	Unhealthy envy.
Therapist:	Would you like me to help you work towards healthy envy rather unhealthy envy?
Client:	That sounds good.

By listening carefully to the client and picking up on things that he doesn't fully understand, the therapist helps himself and the client realise that her real problem is unhealthy envy rather than driving anxiety. As such, the client's original goal was being driven (pardon the pun!) by her feelings of unhealthy envy and that these feelings needed to be targeted for change. As such, the client's new goal was to work towards feeling healthy envy rather than unhealthy envy.

Goals and the Working Alliance: A Final Word

Working alliance theory argues that the strength of the alliance is enhanced and the effectiveness of therapy increased under the following conditions:

1   When the therapist and client agree on the client's goals and these goals are in the client's best long-term interests.
2   When the client actively works towards these goals.

It is important to note in this context that client's goals do change over the course of therapy, partly because of intervening life events and partly because of the work that therapist and client have done to date. It is important, therefore, that the therapist keeps herself up to date on the current state of the client's goals and not assume that once they are expressed, normally at the beginning of therapy, they apply across the therapeutic process.

In the next and closing chapter, I will consider REBT skills in the tasks domain of the working alliance.

7

REBT SKILLS IN THE TASK DOMAIN OF THE WORKING ALLIANCE

Introduction

In this final chapter, I will consider REBT skills in the task domain of the working alliance. The REBT therapist has many tasks to carry out in therapy and I have already discussed and illustrated those which are particularly relevant to the other domains of the working alliance. Thus, in Chapter 4, I considered how the REBT therapist attends to, nurtures and develops the bond between herself and her client. In Chapter 5, I focused on the therapist's tasks in helping her client to understand and discuss their respective views about salient aspects of REBT theory and practice. In Chapter 6, I discussed the therapist's tasks in eliciting the client's goals, which are realistic, achievable and serve as a beacon for the work that the both client and therapist need to do to help the client achieve these goals. Indeed, in my view, therapist and client tasks can best be seen instrumentally as what they both need to do to help the client achieve his therapeutic goals. As this is a book and series on therapist skills, I will focus on these tasks in this chapter. However, there is a growing literature which is devoted to help clients learn, develop and implement the skills of REBT self-therapy and I refer the interested reader to this literature (Dryden, 2001, 2004, 2006a; Grieger & Woods, 1998).

A comprehensive discussion of REBT skills in the tasks domain of the alliance would require an entire book and thus I have chosen to be selective. I have decided not to outline the many techniques that REBT use in the course of therapy since they are readily available elsewhere (e.g. Bernard & Wolfe, 1993; Dryden & Neenan, 2004b). Rather, I have chosen to deal with tasks in a broad way. Thus, I will discuss:

- Assessing clients' problems
- Assessing clients' meta-disturbance
- Helping clients to examine their beliefs
- Negotiating and reviewing homework assignments
- Helping clients to generalise their gains
- Helping clients to identify and examine their doubts, reservations and objections
- Helping clients to prevent relapse
- Ending therapy.

I will not address the whole issue of dealing with obstacles to change because this is a large topic with entire books devoted to it (Ellis, 2002; Neenan & Dryden, 1996). Rather, I will deal with one aspect of this issue, which is particularly relevant to REBT, that is helping clients to identify and examine their doubts, reservations and objections. I will also not deal with the skills involved in helping clients to question their distorted inferences at 'A' and at 'C'. The way that REBT therapists do this is indistinguishable from how other CBT therapists do it, and this skill has been adequately covered in another book in this series (see Wills, 2008). Finally, I will reiterate some of the points I made about tasks and the working alliance in Chapter 3.

Assessing Clients' Problems with Special Reference to Assessing Irrational Beliefs

I pointed out in Chapter 3 that the four domains of the working alliance should not be regarded as separate but rather as interlocking components. Thus, I have already discussed issues pertaining to assessment in Chapter 4, when I discussed the skills of conveying empathy from an REBT perspective, in Chapter 5, when I discussed the skills involved in outlining the REBT view of psychological problems, and in Chapter 6, when I discussed the skills involved in helping clients formulate their problems and goals using the REBT framework.

In those chapters, you will find a discussion of skills related to assessing the context in which a client's problem occurs, the major inference at 'A' made by the client, and the emotional, behavioural and thinking consequences of irrational beliefs. As you will find less material on assessing irrational beliefs in those chapters, I will concentrate on assessment of these beliefs and their rational alternatives in the material that I will now present. In the segment that follows, I will present work from a different therapy, where the therapist is male and the client female.

An Example of Assessing a Client's Problem

Therapist: What problem can I help you with today, Sharon?

Sharon: I'd like to talk about the fact that I often feel ashamed of myself and I really want to do something about it.

Therapist: OK. Can you give me a specific example of this problem?

[Straight away the therapist asks for a specific example of the more general problem articulated by Sharon.]

Sharon: That's easy. It happened yesterday. I was giving a lecture to my students and I said something stupid. I laughed about it at the time but ever since I have been thinking about it and when I do I feel mortified.

(Continued)

(Continued)

Therapist: With shame?

Sharon: Yes.

Therapist: When you feel ashamed about saying that stupid thing, what is it about say-
              ing it that you feel most ashamed of?

*[The therapist is assessing for the client's 'A'. It may be 'saying something stupid' or it
may be something else.]*

Sharon: That I am much better than that.

Therapist: Are you saying that by saying that stupid thing you fell very short of your ideal?

*[Here the therapist's question is informed partly by the client's last response and partly
by REBT's perspective on shame, which says that a common theme in shame at 'A' is
'falling very short of one's ideal'.]*

Sharon: Exactly.

Therapist: So at 'C' in the ABC framework that we have used before, you feel shame and
              your 'A' is that you have fallen very short of your ideal by saying something
              stupid in front of your students. Is that right?

*[Note that the therapist has used the theme 'fallen very short of your ideal' and the exam-
ple of that theme in his response.]*

Sharon: Yes.

Therapist: Now was it you falling short of your ideal that led to your feelings of shame
              or your belief about you falling short?

*[Here the therapist is helping the client make what is known as the B–C connection in
REBT, i.e. that 'C' about 'A' is largely determined by 'B'.]*

Sharon: My belief.

Therapist: So what were you demanding about you falling very short in that way that led
              to your feelings of shame?

*[The therapist has previously helped Sharon to understand the REBT model of psy-
chological problems so he asks Sharon a theory-driven question based on this model
to assess her rigid demand.]*

Sharon: I absolutely should not have said that stupid thing.

Therapist: And how did you evaluate yourself for doing what you absolutely should not
              have done?

[Here the therapist is assessing the client's attitude towards herself.]

Sharon: I am a defective person.

Therapist: And if you fall short in the same way again, what would be a healthier feeling
              alternative?

[Here the therapist is assessing the Sharon's emotional goal.]

Sharon: I'm not sure what to call the feeling.

Therapist: Well, in REBT theory we call it disappointment. So here you would feel really
              disappointed that you fell short of your ideal, but not disappointed in your-
              self for doing so.

Sharon: Yes, that's worth striving for.

Therapist: OK. Now what beliefs would you have to hold that would enable you to do that? Let's take the alternative to your demand first?

[Remember that the therapist has already taught the client the REBT model of psychological disturbance and health.]

Sharon: OK. Let's see. I would prefer it if I had not fallen short of my ideal by saying that stupid thing.

Therapist: That is half of the rational belief...What's the but?

[Sharon has given the 'partial preference' part of the non-dogmatic preference, but did not negate the demand (see Chapter 1, p. 6). So the therapist prompts her.]

Sharon: Oh, OK. I would prefer it if I had not fallen short of my ideal by saying that stupid thing, but I don't have to be exempt from falling short.

Therapist: Excellent, and what would be your self-acceptance belief?

[Again, the therapist is asking a theory-driven question. And remember the therapist has already taught Sharon the model.]

Sharon: I'm a fallible person who fell short of my ideal by saying something silly. I'm not a defective person.

Therapist: And can you see that if you really believe the flexible belief and the self-acceptance belief, then you will feel disappointed, but not ashamed about falling short of your ideal in this way?

Sharon: I do.

A = I have fallen very short of my ideal by saying something stupid in a lecture

iB = I absolutely should not have said fallen short of my ideal by saying that stupid thing

rB = I would prefer it if I had not fallen short of my ideal by saying that stupid thing, but I don't have to be exempt from doing so

= I am a defective person

= I am a fallible person, not a defective one

C = Shame

C (emotional goal) = Disappointment

FIGURE 7.1   *Assessment of Sharon's specific problem and her goal together with the appropriate beliefs*

It is often helpful for the therapist to write the information he elicits from the client during an assessment on a whiteboard. Figure 7.1 shows the assessment of Sharon's specific problem and her goal, together with the appropriate beliefs.

Assessing for Clients' Meta-disturbance

In Chapter 1 (see p. 10), I indicated that focusing on clients' meta-disturbance is a distinctive feature of REBT. If you recall, meta-disturbance occurs when a client disturbs herself about her original disturbance. Here is an example of how Edwin's therapist assessed for the possibility that Edwin experienced meta-disturbance.

> *Therapist:*   When you feel jealous about your wife enjoying the company of an attractive man more than your company how do you feel about feeling jealous?
> *Edwin:*   I feel ashamed about it.
>
> *[This indicates the presence of meta-disturbance. What the therapist does now is to get information from Edwin to determine, from her perspective, whether or not they need to work on Edwin's meta-disturbance before his original disturbance.]*
>
> *Therapist:*   Do you think your feelings of shame will interfere with us working on your jealousy problem in therapy sessions?
> *Edwin:*   I don't think so.
> *Therapist:*   And do you think your shame will interfere with you working on your jealousy problem outside therapy?
> *Edwin:*   No.
> *Therapist:*   Final question. Which do you want to work on first in therapy, your shame or your jealousy?
> *Edwin:*   Definitely my jealousy.

While the therapist has discovered that Edwin has meta-disturbance about his jealousy, they both decide to target his jealousy first because the three major criteria for prioritising his meta-disturbance were not met (see Chapter 1, p. 10).

Helping Clients to Examine their Beliefs

What I call 'examining beliefs' here is more traditionally known 'disputing beliefs' in the REBT literature. DiGiuseppe (1991) has argued that this examining process has a number of steps. It is important to note at the outset that the order in which the therapist carries out these steps is flexible:

1   Formulating the client's irrational belief.
2   Asking the client questions to determine the empirical, logical and pragmatic status of his irrational belief.
3   Constructing the client's rational belief.
4   Asking the client questions to determine the empirical, logical and pragmatic status of his constructed rational belief.
5   Asking the client to commit himself to strengthening his rational belief. If steps 2 and 4 are done skilfully, then the client almost never wants to strengthen his irrational belief, although he may have some doubts about giving up his irrational belief in favour of his newly constructed rational belief (see pp. 102–3 later in this chapter).

I have argued elsewhere that there are a number of different orders in which one can examine a client's belief (Neenan & Dryden, 1999). I also argued in that publication that it is best to examine pairs of beliefs separately (e.g. a demand vs. a non-dogmatic preference separately from a self-depreciation belief vs. a self-acceptance belief).

Therapist Styles in Helping Clients to Examine their Beliefs

DiGiuseppe (1991) has argued that there are a variety of styles which REBT therapists can adopt in helping clients to examine their beliefs. I will briefly describe them here and illustrate the main two (Socratic and didactic) in the example that follows.

The Socratic Style

When using the Socratic style in helping a client to examine his belief, the therapist asks the client questions, the purpose of which is to help the client see for himself why his irrational belief is irrational (i.e. false, illogical and largely unconstructive) and his alternative rational belief is rational (i.e. true, logical and largely constructive). If the client gives an 'incorrect' answer, then the therapist asks another question which helps him to see why his answer is incorrect and which again guides him through further questioning to giving the 'right' answer. The major purpose of Socratic questioning is to encourage clients to think through the issues for themselves before finally gaining intellectual insight into the irrationality of the irrational belief being examined and the rationality of the alternative rational belief (see Chapter 5, pp. 60–1 and the next section).

While REBT therapists prefer, in general, to use the Socratic style of helping clients to examine their beliefs, they appreciate that not all clients will benefit from engaging in Socratic examination. Some clients will not benefit from this style at all because they find it difficult to examine abstract concepts in a fairly open-ended manner, and other clients may be able to benefit in the main from the Socratic style but get stuck with this style on particular issues. In such cases, it is likely that the therapists will employ the didactic style of helping clients to examine their beliefs.

The Didactic Style

When a therapist is employing the didactic style of helping a client to examine his beliefs, the therapist explains by making declarative points about why the client's irrational belief is irrational (i.e. false, illogical and largely unconstructive) and why his alternative rational belief is rational (i.e. true, logical and largely constructive). When using the didactic style, the skilful REBT therapist will:

1   Make her didactic points short. She will particularly guard against providing the client with too much material.
2   Take into account the learning style of the client and use words that will help the client to digest the material presented and talk at a rate that will promote rather than impede client learning.
3   Ensure that the client understands the point that the therapist has made. To this end the therapist asks the client to put into his own words the point being made. The therapist will reiterate any point that the client has not grasped using a different explanation until the client has understood it.

4   Elicit the client's view of the point being made once the client has understood the point. The skilful REBT therapist knows that a client can understand a point correctly, but still disagree with it.
5   Engage the client in a productive dialogue when the client indicates that he disagrees with a point that the therapist has didactically taught. During this dialogue the therapist will attempt to address and correct any misconceptions that the client has revealed and does so while conveying empathy and acceptance of the client.

While using the didactic style, and indeed other styles of helping clients to examine their irrational beliefs, the skilful REBT therapist rigorously guards against believing that she has to get the client to think irrationally. This, of course, would be an irrational stance to take!

The Metaphorical Style

When a therapist adopts a metaphorical style in helping clients to examine their beliefs, she will use a metaphor or tell a story which demonstrates a rational point. After doing so, it is important for the therapist to check that the client has understood the point otherwise there is a danger that the client will have not learned the principle intended.

Here is an example of such a metaphor. In the following segment the therapist will tell a story designed to show the futility of holding rigid demands about issues outside the client's control (which is the client's problem). A certain amount of poetic licence is taken with the story to make the intended point.

Therapist: Do you know the story of King Canute?
Client: I think so.
Therapist: Well let me remind you because it is relevant to what we have been talking about. OK?
Client: Fine
Therapist: Well, King Canute had a preference for the tide to come in when he wanted it to come in and for it to go out when he wanted it to go out. He then had a choice. He could either make that preference flexible by saying something like: 'I'd like the tide to follow my wishes, but sadly it doesn't have to do so' or he could transform his preference into a rigid belief: 'I'd like the tide to follow my wishes and therefore because I am King it has to do so'. Well, suffice it to say King Canute held the rigid belief. What do you think happened to the tide as a result of the king's demand?
Client: Nothing.
Therapist: Do you know why?
Client: Because the tide's comings and goings are not determined by the demands of a king.
Therapist: Or anyone else's come to that. Now what happened to the king as a result of his demand?
Client: He got furious?
Therapist: So what is the moral of this story?

[Having told the story, the therapist checked with the client that he understood the point.]

Client:	That holding a demand about something outside your control only makes you furious and doesn't change the thing you are making a demand about.
Therapist:	Excellent. Now let's apply this point to what we have been discussing.

The Use of Humour in Helping Clients to Examine Beliefs

While the use of humour is not really a style of examining beliefs in itself, the therapist can introduce humour into whatever style she is currently adopting. It is notoriously difficult to capture humour on the written page since much of its effect depends on the tone of voice of the therapist and the manner and style of delivery. However, here is how the therapist who told the story of King Canute to her client could have introduced humour into her metaphorical style.

Therapist:	... What do you think happened to the tide as a result of the king's demand?
Client:	Nothing.
Therapist:	Actually, you are wrong. The tide said: We are usually guided by the moon and we are supposed to be going out now, but the king is demanding that we come in so lads, about turn!
Client:	Very amusing.
Therapist:	But what point do you think I'm making?
Client:	That holding a demand about something outside your control doesn't change the thing you are making a demand about.
Therapist:	Even if you are a king?
Client:	Even then.

The Purpose of Examining Beliefs

In Chapter 5, I distinguished between intellectual insight and emotional insight. I showed that intellectual insight is an intellectual understanding that irrational beliefs are irrational and that rational beliefs are rational, but that this understanding does not yet have a healthy impact on the client's emotions, behaviour and subsequent thinking. Emotional insight, on the other hand, is a deep, emotionally-based conviction which does have a healthy impact on the client's feelings and behaviour (Ellis, 1963). In my view, the purpose of intellectual insight is to promote a cognitive understanding and it is important to help clients realise this point. I refer you to the tennis analogy I presented in Chapter 5 (pp. 61–3) which makes this very point (among others). Although it does not change feelings, etc., intellectual insight is important in that it provides the cognitive underpinnings for the work that the client needs to do in order to achieve emotional insight. Without that roadmap, the client would be like a house without proper foundations!

An Example of Helping a Client Examine her Beliefs

In the following example, the therapist is using empirical and pragmatic arguments with the client when helping her to examine (a) her rigid demand and her non-dogmatic preference, and (b) her self-depreciation belief and her self-acceptance belief. You will see that these two pairs of beliefs are taken separately. There are other orders for examining or disputing beliefs (see Neenan & Dryden, 1999).

It is important to note that different clients find different arguments persuasive. In the example that follows, the therapist has already ascertained from previous experience that his client did not find logical arguments persuasive and thus he has not used them here. For information concerning how to use logical arguments in the belief examining process, consult Dryden (2001, 2009b).

Therapist: So let's go on to examining both sets of beliefs. OK?
Sharon: Fine.

[Because demands and non-dogmatic preferences are the most central of all irrational beliefs (see Chapter 1) it follows that REBT therapists often suggest starting with examining these beliefs.]

Therapist: Let's take them one at a time and let me write them on the board because it would be easier to examine them that way (writes them up on the board). Let's look at the demand and non-dogmatic preference first.

Demand	Non-dogmatic Preference
iB = I absolutely should not have said fallen short of my ideal by saying that stupid thing.	rB = I would prefer it if I had not fallen short of my ideal by saying that stupid thing, but I don't have to be exempt from doing so.

Therapist: Now, looking at those two beliefs, which is true and which is false?
Sharon: Well, my demand is obviously false.

[In this type of examining belief when the client provides the correct answer, the therapist follows by asking the client why it is correct.]

Therapist: Why is it false?
Sharon: Well, if it was true then I could not have possibly fallen short of my ideal and said what I said.

Therapist: Why?
Client: Well, the law of nature that decreed that I must not do it would have prevented me.
Therapist: I just had an image of you trying to fall short of your ideal and saying something stupid and that law of nature stopping you. You literally could not get the words out of your mouth, could you?

[The therapist adds a little humour to his Socratic style.]

Sharon [laughing]: No, I guess I couldn't!
Therapist: So what's the relationship between your demand and freedom of speech and action?

[The therapist is now subtly switching to investigate the consequences of holding the demand. This is the pragmatic argument.]

Sharon:	It robs me of my freedom to fall short of my ideal and to say stupid things.
Therapist:	And would you like to live in a world that deprives you of such basic freedoms?
Sharon:	No, you are right, I wouldn't. I hadn't looked at it like that before.
Therapist:	So if your demand existed, then you would have to campaign for the restoration of your freedom to fall short of your ideal and to say stupid things!

[Another attempt of humour.]

Sharon:	I can imagine writing the banner right now.

[Sharon responds well to the humour.]

Therapist:	'What do I want? My freedom to be stupid. When do I want it? Fish!'

[The therapist's humour is turning surreal to show that even her banner can say something stupid.]

Sharon:	Très amusant.

[Sharon gets the point.]

Therapist:	Seriously, though, apart from the loss of the freedom of speech and action, what are the other consequences of your demand?
Sharon:	I experience shame and that is a really painful emotion.
Therapist:	Anything else?
Sharon:	I'm not sure?
Therapist:	Well, how much time did you spend thinking about what you said afterwards?
Sharon:	Oh, I thought about it on and off ever since, more on than off.
Therapist:	So, you were preoccupied with it?
Sharon:	Yes, very much so.
Therapist:	What impact does it have on your behaviour?
Sharon:	It leads me to over-prepare my lectures. I spend too much time trying to ensure that I don't say anything stupid. I stop short of writing my lectures verbatim, but I'm getting to that point.
Therapist:	Can you summarise what we have covered so far?
Sharon:	My demand is false and has a number of unfortunate consequences. It deprives me of basic human freedoms – to fall short of my ideal and to say stupid things – it leads to painful feelings of shame. It leads me to be preoccupied with what I said and also leads me to over-preparing my lectures and to think seriously about writing my lectures so that I read them word for word, thus attempting to ensure that I don't say anything stupid.
Therapist:	That is an excellent summary. Now let's consider your non-dogmatic preference. Is it true or false?

(Continued)

(Continued)

[The therapist again begins with the empirical question.]

Sharon:	It's true.
Therapist:	What's the reason for your answer?
Sharon:	Well, it's true that I would have preferred not to have fallen short of my ideal by saying that stupid thing, and it's also true that I don't have to be exempt from falling short in this way. The fact that I did so proves that.
Therapist:	What impact does your non-dogmatic preference have on your freedom to say and do stupid things?

[The therapist now moves on to pragmatic questioning and will use pragmatic questions to contrast every dysfunctional consequence of the demand with the more functional alternative consequence of the non-dogmatic preference.]

Sharon:	It preserves it.
Therapist:	A pity, I was looking forward to seeing that banner on the streets of London! Now what impact would your rational belief have on your feelings?
Sharon:	As we said before, I would feel disappointed.
Therapist:	But not ashamed, right?
Sharon:	No. Not ashamed.
Therapist:	Now, what impact would your rational belief have on how much time you would think about the stupid thing you said at the lecture?
Sharon:	Well, I would think about it from time to time but far less than I actually did.
Therapist:	And the impact of the belief on how much you would prepare for the next lecture?
Sharon:	Well, I would still prepare for the lecture, but I wouldn't over-prepare for it. And I certainly wouldn't write it all down to be read verbatim at the lecture.
Therapist:	Can you sum up?
Sharon:	My non-dogmatic preference is true and has better consequences for me. It preserves my freedom to fall short of my ideal and to say stupid things. It would lead me to feel disappointment rather than shame and it would lead me to think of what I said occasionally rather than be preoccupied with it. Finally, the belief would lead me to prepare reasonably for the lecture rather than to over-prepare for it.
Therapist:	Another great summary. So, which belief would you like to commit yourself to?
Sharon:	My non-dogmatic preference.

[The therapist now moves to examining the client's self-depreciation and self-acceptance beliefs.]

Therapist:	Now let's examine your self-depreciation and self-acceptance beliefs there up on the board.

Self-depreciation belief	Self-acceptance belief
I am a defective person	I am a fallible person, not a defective one

Therapist:	Which of these beliefs is true and which is false?
Sharon:	The self-acceptance belief is true and the self-depreciation belief is false.
Therapist:	Why is that?
Sharon:	Well, I am not defective.
Therapist:	Can you prove that?
Sharon:	I can't put it into words.

[As Sharon is struggling with the therapist's Socratic style on this point, so the therapist decided to make his point didactically.]

Therapist:	Well, if you were defective as a person, everything would be defective about you. Is that true of you?
Sharon:	No plenty of things about me 'work'!
Therapist:	And why is it true that you are fallible?

[After a brief didactic point, the therapist resumes his Socratic style.]

Sharon:	Well fallible means prone to error and that's me as well as other humans.
Therapist:	OK, let's look at the consequences of both beliefs ...

It often occurs that the derivatives of rigid beliefs and flexible beliefs (in Sharon's case, a self-depreciation belief and a self-acceptance belief) have the same consequences as the rigid and flexible beliefs themselves. As such, I will omit the relevant dialogue on this point as it mirrored the discussion that the therapist and Sharon had on the emotional, thinking and behavioural consequences of her rigid demand and non-dogmatic preference. At the end of this particular sequence, Sharon said that she wanted to commit herself to her self-acceptance belief.

Negotiating and Reviewing Homework Assignments

Once the client has achieved intellectual insight into his irrational and rational beliefs, he is ready to begin to move towards emotional insight and meaningful change. In order to do this, he needs to put into practice in his everyday life what he has learned in therapy. The therapist aids this process by negotiating suitable homework assignments at the end of a session and reviewing them at the beginning of the following session. If she does this rigorously, then her client is more likely to do homework assignments than if she is haphazard about doing so. Research shows that regular completion of homework assignments in the cognitive-behavioural therapies is a powerful predictor of a good therapeutic outcome for clients (e.g. Burns & Spangler, 2000).

Negotiating Homework Assignments

A skilful REBT therapist does the following with respect to negotiating a suitable homework assignment with her client. She:

- Involves the client fully in the homework negotiation process
- Gives herself sufficient time to negotiate an appropriate assignment at the end of the therapy session
- Negotiates an assignment that follows logically from the work done in the session
- Ensures that the client understands the purpose of doing the assignment and how doing it will help him to achieve his goals
- Negotiates whenever possible an assignment that allows the client to rehearse a rational belief while acting and thinking in ways that are consistent with this rational belief
- Ensures that the client has the ability and the skills to do the assignment
- Elicits a commitment from the client to do the homework assignment rather than to try to do it
- Encourages the client to specify when and where he will carry out the assignment
- Helps the client to identify and deal with obstacles to homework completion
- Helps the client to identify behaviours that are designed to keep him safe while he is carrying out the assignment and encourage him to refrain from using these safety-seeking strategies
- Rehearses the homework assignment with the client in the therapy session either in role play or imagery
- Encourages the client to make a written note of the homework assignment, its purpose and where and when he is going to do it.

An Example of Negotiating Homework with a Client

In this example of negotiating a homework assignment, the therapist had helped Edwin in a previous session to put his general problem and related goal into the REBT framework (see Chapter 6, pp. 68–70). In the current session she has assessed the specific example of his problem where he felt jealous of his wife laughing and joking with Gavin at a dinner party, examined his irrational and rational belief and elicited a commitment from him that he wanted to commit himself to strengthening his rational belief which was. 'I really don't want my wife to enjoy Gavin's company more than mine, but she doesn't have to do what I want'. The therapist has given herself about 12 minutes to negotiate a suitable homework assignment with Edwin that follows logically from the work that they have done in the session and that is related to the general problem that they formulated in the previous session. We pick up the dialogue at this point.

Therapist:	Now we need to help you to practise your rational belief, namely: 'I really don't want my wife to enjoy an attractive man's company more than mine, but she doesn't have to do what I want'. Can you think of ways you can practise that belief before our session next week?
Edwin:	Well, my wife and I have a couple of social events to go to this weekend. My wife is very sociable and quite attractive, so attractive guys usually do talk to her and I do routinely feel jealous when they do.
Therapist:	Now, when we formulated your goal we developed some alternative healthy behaviour that you could engage in which is consistent with your rational belief. Can you remember what that was?

Edwin:	Talking to someone else without checking on my wife.
Therapist:	Now you may still feel the urge to take your wife home or to try to get her to talk to you rather than to him.

[*Here the therapist raises the possibility that Edwin may have the urge to seek safety in the situation and will suggest a way of dealing with it.*]

Edwin:	I know. How can I deal with these urges?
Therapist:	Well, I suggest that you don't suppress them since suppressing urges can actually strengthen them.
Edwin:	Tell me about it.
Therapist:	Instead, I suggest that you notice the urge, let it be and concentrate on who you are talking to. OK?

[*This is an important point. Urges to act and think unconstructively will remain even when the client is rehearsing his rational belief and acting on this belief. As the therapist says, accepting the urge without engaging in it or suppressing it and continuing to act and think healthily is probably the best way to deal with such urges.*]

Edwin:	OK.
Therapist:	Apart from rehearsing your rational belief from time to time, there was some other thinking that you were going to engage in. Do you remember what that was?
Edwin:	Let me look in my notebook .... I am going to think that my wife is enjoying the guy's company and that's all it means in all probability.
Therapist:	Excellent. Again, you will still have your old thought that the guy will take your wife away from you and the picture of them having sex coming into your mind, but if they do, just let come and don't try to suppress them on the one hand or engage with them on the other. Once or twice, you can rehearse your new thought that your wife is enjoying the guy's company and that's all it means in all probability while you continue to talk to whomever you are talking to.

[*Here the therapist is showing Edwin how to deal with his old thought and picture coming into his mind. The therapist is aware that if Edwin engages with or tries to suppress these cognitions, then they will interfere with him deepening his conviction in his rational belief.*]

Therapist:	Can you think of any obstacles that might prevent you from doing this homework twice over the weekend?
Edwin:	No, I'm determined to do it.
Therapist:	OK, one more thing. Your feelings may not change for a while until you have put plenty of thinking and behavioural practice into the bank, as it were.

[*Here the therapist is addressing an obstacle to the continued execution of homework assignments. Namely that feelings change after much practice of healthy thinking (at the belief and the inferential levels) and constructive action. Unless the client understands, he may get discouraged and give up the practice.*]

Edwin:	So it's like an account where I make lots of deposits and get delayed interest.
Therapist:	Yes, that is a really good way of putting it. Before you go, why not make a note of the homework in your notebook.
Edwin [writing]:	Good idea.
Therapist:	See you next week.

Reviewing Homework Assignments

A skilful REBT therapist does the following with respect to reviewing her client's homework assignment with him in the following session. She:

- Ensures that she does review the homework assignment with the client
- Checks that the client has done the homework assignment in full and explores reasons why he did not do some of the homework
- Explores with the client the reasons why he made any modifications to the homework assignment, then she deals with these reasons
- Checks with the client what he learned from doing the assignment, assuming that he did it in full
- Explores with the client why he did not do the homework assignment (in part or in full) and deals with these reasons
- Helps the client to capitalise on his success in doing the assignment
- Helps the client to deal rationally with any failures encountered in doing the assignment
- Corrects any errors that the client made or misconceptions that the client expressed.

An Example of Reviewing Homework with a Client

In the following segment, the therapist reviews Edwin's homework which she negotiated with him the week before.

Therapist:	OK, that's our agenda set up for today. Let's start by looking at how the homework went.
Edwin:	Like the curate's egg, good in parts.
Therapist:	Shall we take it in the order that you did it?
Edwin:	OK. Well, Friday night went very well.
Therapist:	Tell me all about it.
Edwin:	Well, we went to a sherry evening at Jim and Marjorie's and although I thought I would know everybody there, I didn't know this one couple, Keith and Samantha, who had just moved into the area. Anyway, Keith's a good looking guy and I could feel myself get jealous when he started talking to Linda. I then rehearsed my rational belief saying I don't like this, but if she enjoys his company more than mine tonight, it's not forbidden...

[Note that Edwin changed the wording of his rational belief, but preserved its meaning. This is a good sign that he is connecting with the meaning of the rational belief rather than just connecting with its expression.]

	... She was smiling and laughing as she usually does, but I talked to Samantha without checking on Linda. The old thoughts and images didn't come and I went home on a high. I didn't get the usual urge to cross-examine Linda that night. I think I told you that I don't act on that urge any more because Linda gets furious when I do so. But I was really surprised that I didn't even get the urge.
Therapist:	So you rehearsed your rational belief and acted accordingly on Friday night and most of the urges didn't come.
Edwin:	That's right. I was really surprised, but mainly pleased.
Therapist:	OK. I particularly liked the fact that you varied the wording of your rational belief, but preserved its meaning.

Edwin:	Thanks. I think I'm getting the hang of that.
Therapist:	Did you prepare yourself before the evening?
Edwin:	Yes. I went over the rational belief and resolved to act in the way we discussed. So, yes, I felt prepared.
Therapist:	OK. So let's deal with the bad part of the curate's egg.
Edwin:	OK. So on Saturday night we had a party to go to and I was sure that there would be plenty of opportunity to practise, but hardly anybody was there. It was a really sad affair and it turned out that the hosts had had a really bad row and cancelled the party but did not get round to phoning everyone. So there was a tense atmosphere, but people sensed what was happening and drifted off. I was annoyed more for the fact that I had prepared myself to practise at the party and did not have the opportunity to do so.
	Anyway, it was about 9pm when we left and Linda and I decided to go to the pub for a drink. At the pub there were a couple of my work colleagues, Peter and his wife Sarah and Mary and her new boyfriend Mark. Now Mark is a handsome devil and I started to get the jealous feelings which was a cue for me to go over my rational belief. So, I reminded myself that Linda is allowed to enjoy Mark's company more than mine that night and I got engaged in conversation with Mary while Linda laughed and joked with Mark. But then I started to actually check on them and I got really mad for giving into the urge … and when I got mad, I got more jealous, then the thoughts came and I engaged with them and the whole thing fell apart. I had the urge to cross-examine Linda when we got home but did not do it, luckily. But I was really annoyed with myself.
Therapist:	OK, so that gives me some clues as to what happened. Obviously, it's good when your homework goes well, but in a strange way it's valuable when it doesn't because it gives us a chance to learn more about the factors associated with the problem and in this case the factors associated with obstacles to getting over the problem. Do you see what I mean?

[Here the therapist touches on what some therapists call the 'win-win' nature of homework assignments. It's good when it goes well and it's good when it doesn't because we can learn more.]

Edwin:	That's an interesting way of looking at it.
Therapist:	Well, it seemed to me that it is when you got mad with yourself that the problems started. Is that right?
Edwin:	Yes.
Therapist:	So shall we zero in on the point at which you started to get mad with yourself?

[The therapist is now suggesting that they get very specific and assess the source of the difficulty.]

Edwin:	OK.
Therapist:	So what were you mad with yourself about?

[The therapist is now doing an ABC assessment of the point when Edwin began to get into trouble.]

Edwin:	I was mad with myself for acting on my urge to check.

(Continued)

(Continued)

[This is Edwin's 'A' in the ABC of the breakdown of his second homework practice. 'C' is his feelings of anger towards himself.]

Therapist: So you were angry at yourself for acting on the urge to check on your wife and it sounded like the kind of anger that led to things falling apart for you homework-wise.

Edwin: Yes it was.

[The therapist is reasonably sure that Edwin's self-anger is unhealthy, but wants to double-check with him before proceeding.]

Edwin: Yes it was.

Therapist: So what were you demanding of yourself?

[The therapist is now assessing Edwin's demand that underpins his self-anger. Note the theory-driven question.]

Edwin: I was demanding that I must not act on that urge.

Therapist: Can you stand back and examine that demand?

Edwin: It's ridiculous because while I may not want to do it, I don't have to perfectly put into practice everything you teach me.

Therapist: What do you think would have happened if you had thought rationally about acting on your urge to check?

[Here the therapist is assessing the potential consequences of this rational belief.]

Edwin: I would have been disappointed, but I would have reminded myself that I don't have to be perfect in doing my homework. Also I would have noted that I don't have to act on this urge, no matter how strong, and gone back to the homework.

[Edwin sees that if he had responded to his lapse rationally, he could have challenged the irrational belief that led to the lapse in the first place (e.g. 'Because I really want to check on my wife, I have to do so').]

Therapist: Both points are excellent, Edwin. Incidentally, do you remember the tennis analogy?

Edwin: Yes.

Therapist: Do you remember the part where you come to practise the new stroke when you feel the urge to play the old stroke?

Edwin: Yes, I remember that.

Therapist: When you feel that urge, is it possible that you might act on it?

Edwin: Of course.

Therapist: The point is if you accept that lapsing back into old habits is an inevitable part of change of any kind, then you can learn from your lapses without self-disturbance. Then you can work on minimising the old strokes and maximising the new strokes.

[Here the therapist makes her point didactically because she is aware that they have a lot to cover in the session and making this point in a didactic way speeds up the process.]

Edwin [*writes*]:	I'm making a note of that in my therapy notebook.
Therapist:	What have you written?

[The therapist is, in effect, checking that Edwin has understood her didactic point.]

Edwin:	Acting on old urges is an inevitable part of change. My job is to learn and minimise such actions, not to condemn myself for them.

Helping Clients to Generalise their Gains

I once had the following experience earlier in my career as an REBT thera-pist. I had been working with a client on his fear of being criticised by his boss. We assessed an example of this problem, identified and examined his beliefs and he committed himself to practising his rational belief and acting in ways consistent with his belief. He did his homework assignment and was very pleased with the results. After reviewing his homework he went on to tell me of an incident after he did his homework. It emerged that he disturbed himself about the prospect of being criticised by a good friend of his. It was clear that the cognitive–emotive–behavioural dynamics of this episode was the same as with his boss, so I pointed this out and asked him if he applied to this episode what he applied with his boss. The client replied that he hadn't and then said something that has stayed with me and has guided my practice as an REBT therapist ever since. He said that he didn't do this because it had not occurred to him to do so. This taught me an important lesson: *Do not leave generalisation to chance in REBT. Deliberately address it as an issue.*

There are a number of ways of doing this and I will list them here, detail the skills involved and provide a couple of illustrations of these skills in action.

Helping Clients to Generalise Gains from a Specific Example of his Problem to Other Examples of His Problems where the Theme of 'A' is the Same

The case that I discussed above, which sensitised me to the issue of helping clients to generalise their gains, was a specific example of this particular issue. It never occurred to my client to generalise his learning from one situation to another because I did not alert him to the importance of doing so.

Learning from this experience, this is what I could have done, and ideally should have done.

Windy:	OK, Ben, so now you can see that you are anxious about being criticised by your boss because you demand that he must not criticise you, and if he does it proves that you are worthless. Together we have developed this alternative rational belief: 'I would prefer it if my boss does not criticise me, but he doesn't have to comply with my wishes. If he criticises me, it does not prove that I am worthless. I am a fallible human being who may or may

(Continued)

(Continued)

not have done something that merits his criticism.' Is that an accurate summary of the work we have done on your beliefs today?

Ben:　　Yes, it is.

Windy:　Now Ben, you have agreed to practise rehearsing this belief while showing your boss the draft report you have been working on. Let me ask you a question. Are you anxious about being criticised by other people as well?

[This is the point where I introduce the topic of generalising gains.]

Ben:　　Yes, I am. I tend to be anxious about being criticised across the board.

Windy:　In addition to the homework that you have agreed to do with your boss, I wonder if you rehearse your new rational belief in other situations where you might be criticised.

Ben:　　That's a great idea. How do I do it?

Windy:　Well, you just adjust the content to the new situation. Have you got an example of where you might be criticised by someone other than your boss before next week's session?

Ben:　　Well I am seeing a good friend of mine who tends to be critical.

Windy:　OK, so have a go at formulating a rational belief about being criticised by your good friend.

[Note that I encourage Ben to be active in coming up with the rational belief. I resist the urge to do this for him.]

Ben:　　OK, here goes: 'I would prefer it if my friend does not criticise me, but he doesn't have to do what I want him to do. If he criticises me, I am still the same fallible human being as I would be if he does not criticise me. I may deserve his criticism or I may not.'

Windy:　Ben, that is really excellent.

Ben:　　Thanks for pointing out the need to generalise what I learned. It would never have occurred to me!

Windy:　Remember that you can practise a version of this belief whenever you are criticised or think you will be.

Ben:　　Good advice!

It would have been interesting to see if Ben had dealt better with being criticised by his friend if I had worked with him to be prepared to generalise his learning, as in the above segment.

Helping Clients to Identify and Examine their Core Beliefs and Rehearse and Act in Ways that are Consistent with Specific Examples of these Beliefs

What is a Core Belief?

A core belief is a general belief that accounts for the person's emotions, behaviours and thinking in a variety of situations related to the theme made explicit in the belief. When these responses are unhealthy, then the belief is known as a core irrational belief. When this is the case, a goal is to help the client formulate and work towards internalising an alternative belief known as a core rational belief.

A core irrational belief derived in this way is bounded by the contexts specified in the formulated problem. If a context is not specified, then the core irrational belief is likely to be more general than if a context is specified.

How to Identify a Core Irrational Belief

The skills involved in helping the client to identify a core irrational belief are as follows.

Using the client's REBT formulated problem list for evidence of the existence of a core irrational belief

It is possible to hypothesise the existence of a core irrational belief just by referring to this list.

For example, in Chapter 6 I presented this formulated client problem: 'Whenever I have to give a talk in public, I get anxious about saying something foolish. So I over-prepare my material and drink alcohol before the talk to calm myself.' The hypothesis is that the client's core irrational belief is: 'I must not say anything foolish when I give a talk in public and I am a fool if I do'. Note that if the formulated problem made no mention of the context (i.e. giving a talk in public, then the core irrational belief would have been even more general (i.e. 'I must not say anything foolish and I am a fool if I do').

As with other hypotheses, a hypothesised core irrational belief derived in this way needs to be confirmed or disconfirmed by the client. If it is confirmed by the client, he needs to rephrase the belief in his own words. Then the client needs to be helped to formulate the alternative core rational belief. Thus: 'I would prefer not to say anything foolish when I give a talk in public, but that doesn't mean that I must not do so. I am not a fool if I do, just a fallible human being who says foolish things from time to time.' Again the client needs to put this core rational belief into his own words.

Keeping a note of theme-related situations the client refers to when discussing problems

If a client keeps bringing up situations with the same theme, then this is evidence that he may have a core irrational belief which can be formulated, discussed with the client and reworded by him. The same is true for the alternative core rational belief. Thus, if the client keeps talking about problems where the theme at 'A' is acting foolishly, then it is possible that he holds a core irrational belief such as 'I must not act foolishly and I am a fool if I do'. If so, then his core rational belief is 'I would prefer not to act foolishly, but that does not mean that I must not do so'.

Helping a Client to Examine Core Beliefs

Helping a client to examine his core irrational and rational beliefs is done in the same way as helping him to examine his specific beliefs. As with the latter, the emphasis is on the use of a variety of styles (i.e. Socratic, didactic and metaphorical) and the use of empirical, logical and pragmatic arguments.

Helping a Client to Act and Think in Ways Consistent with his Core Rational Belief

When helping a client to act and think in ways that are consistent with his core rational belief, the therapist does the following:

1   Have the client take this as his core rational belief.
2   Have him then specify relevant situations that are specific representations of the context and theme specified in this belief.
3   Have him formulate a specific version of his core rational belief that he can rehearse in these situations.
4   Have him specify behaviours and thoughts that are consequences of these specific rational beliefs.
5   Encourage him to put these behaviours and thoughts into practice in relevant situations while rehearsing the specific rational belief and review the results.

Helping Clients to Identify and Examine Their Doubts, Reservations and Objections

As I have shown throughout this book, the skilful REBT therapist is very explicit about aspects of REBT theory and practice that are relevant to the client's therapy. Because the skilful REBT therapist often asks for her client's understanding, she also creates for her client many opportunities for the client to voice his doubts, reservations and objections (henceforth known as DROs) about the material that he has presented. At other times the therapist has a sense that her client might have a DRO from the tone of his voice or from his non-verbal behaviour, and if this is the case she has the option to express her impression or refer the matter more formally to the reflection process (see Chapter 4, pp. 30–1).

The client may have DROs about a number of different issues. Here is a list of common DROs:

- DROs about giving up irrational beliefs in favour of rational beliefs
- DROs about moving away from unhealthy negation emotions (UNEs) in favour of healthy negative emotions (HNEs)
- DROs about acting in ways deemed constructive by REBT theory rather than acting in ways deemed unconstructive by the theory.

It is worth noting that many DROs are based on clients' misconceptions of the points that have been made to them, as will be illustrated below.

However, first, I will outline the therapist skills needed when dealing effectively with a DRO. In doing so, I will assume that the therapist senses correctly that the client has a DRO, but has not expressed it.

1   The therapist senses that the client may be holding a DRO.
2   She expresses this sense to the client and invites the client to comment.
3   The client expresses the DRO (if he has one).
4   The therapist invites elaboration and conveys empathy with the client's position.
5   The therapist privately notes the problem with the client's DRO.
6   The therapist invites the client to hear her view of the client's DRO.

7   If the client accepts the invitation, the therapist expresses her view (if the client does not accept the invitation, the therapist refers this to the reflection process for discussion).

8   The therapist engages the client in a discussion until the DRO is effectively addressed.

An Example of How to Identify and Deal with a Client's Doubt, Reservation or Objection

In the following segment, Harry's therapist has assessed a specific example of his unhealthy anger problem. In particular, she has helped Harry to see that the irrational belief that underpinned his anger was 'My employee absolutely should not have left early without permission and he is a bad person for doing so'. The therapist has helped Harry examine his demand and non-dogmatic preference and is proceeding to help him examine his other-depreciation belief and other-acceptance belief.

Therapist: Now let's consider your other-depreciation belief and your other-acceptance belief?

Harry: OK. ...

Therapist: You look a bit reticent.

[The therapist communicates her sense that the client is uneasy about something.]

Harry: Well, I'm not sure I want to accept my employee.

[The client mentions his DRO.]

Therapist: Why's that?

[The therapist asks Harry to elaborate on his DRO.]

Harry: Acceptance sounds as though I am condoning his behaviour.

[Harry has now expressed his DRO in full.]

Therapist: I can really understand that you don't want to condone your employee's behaviour and if other-acceptance meant that, I would not encourage you to do so. Would it help if I explain what other-acceptance means?

[The therapist empathises with Harry's wish not to condone his employee's behaviour and asks Harry if he wants to hear her view of the client's DRO.]

Harry: OK.

[Harry accepts the therapist's invitation.]

Therapist: Well, in my view, in this instance, an other-acceptance belief indicates that your employee acted very badly and should take the consequences for his actions, but it also says that he is not a bad person, but a fallible person who acted badly. He should be penalised but not damned. What do you think?

[The therapist expresses her view.]

Harry: That deals with my reservation. I can go along with that!

[The therapist has effectively addressed Harry's DRO.]

Helping Clients to Prevent Relapse

The concept of relapse prevention emerged from the field of addiction treatment, but has since been more widely applied in the field of counselling and psychotherapy (Marlatt & Donovan, 2005). While a full discussion of how REBT therapists help their clients to prevent relapse merits an entire volume, and thus is beyond the scope of this present work, in keeping with the focus of this book on skills, I will outline the skills that REBT therapists need to display in helping clients in this area. Before I proceed, I wish to distinguish between a lapse and a relapse. I see a lapse as a time-limited setback that occurs in the course of overall progress made by the client. It reflects the fact that a client is a human being rather than a programmable robot and, as such, is prone to error and lapsing. It is rare for a client to make perfect progress and not lapse at some point in the therapeutic process. Indeed, most clients will lapse more than once. You will note therefore that this section is called 'Helping clients to prevent relapse' and not 'Helping clients to prevent lapses'. The latter would be perfectionistic and unrealistic. As we will see, a more appropriate goal is to help clients learn from their lapses and minimise (rather than prevent) their occurrence.

On the other hand, a relapse is a return to the state where the client was before seeking help. It is often thought of by clients as 'going back to square one'. It often transpires that a relapse occurs because a client has disturbed himself about a lapse, not dealt with that disturbance and therefore not learned from the lapse. When this is accompanied by the person abandoning his commitment to self-change, then he is at an increased risk of relapse.

Identifying and Dealing with a Client's Vulnerability Factors

An important part of relapse prevention on a client problem is helping the client to identify and deal with factors that render him vulnerable to experiencing the problem again without coping with it (I call these 'vulnerability factors'). These might be factors external to the person (e.g. environmental factors, how others treat the client) or internal to the client (e.g. the client's mood, feelings, thoughts or urges to act). The point is that if the client encounters or experiences the factor, this renders him vulnerable to experiencing his problem without coping with it. Here are the skills that the REBT therapist needs to demonstrate if she is to help the client deal effectively with his vulnerability factors.

Providing a Rationale for Identifying and Dealing with Vulnerability Factors

As in other cases, it is useful for the therapist to provide the client with a rationale for dealing with his vulnerability factors. In this way the client understands what the therapist plans to do and is able to give (or withhold) consent to proceed. In the following segment, the therapist is working with Edwin and has put the issue of dealing with vulnerability factors on the session agenda (see Chapter 4, pp. 27–30). The time has come for the therapist in introduce the topic to Edwin.

Therapist:	I put the topic of dealing with vulnerability factors on the agenda, because I think we are ready to deal with them in therapy. Would you agree that you have made quite a bit of progress in dealing with your jealousy in therapy?
Edwin:	I would agree with that. I'm pleased with what I have achieved so far.
Therapist:	Now vulnerability factors are what they sound like, factors that render you vulnerable – not to you feeling jealous because you have had that experience and dealt with it, but to you feeling jealous and not dealing with it. These factors can be situational, something to do with other people or factors inside you, like thoughts or feelings or urges to act in a certain way. Does that make sense?
Edwin:	Kind of. You mean like factors that, if they exist, would make it really difficult for me to deal with my jealous feelings?
Therapist:	Exactly.
Edwin:	Yes it would be very sensible for us to identify and deal with these.

Helping the Client to Identify Vulnerability Factors and Specify a Provisional Working Order

The first step in assisting the client to deal with his vulnerability factors is to help him identify these vulnerability factors, both external and internal. These may come readily to the client's mind or, if not, it is worthwhile asking the client if he is avoiding any relevant external and/or internal factors that, if he were to confront them, would render him vulnerable to experiencing his problem without dealing with it.

Therapist:	OK, let's make a start by identifying such factors. What comes to mind when you think of factors that might render you vulnerable in the way we have defined them?
Edwin:	Well, one thing that comes to mind is a sense of me feeling that I've cracked the problem so I stop using the skills that you have taught me.
Therapist:	OK, so that's internal factor. I'll make a list on the board and write that down ... [*writes on the board*] ... what else?
Edwin:	Well, two external factors come to mind. One is with a guy called Philip. I know my wife fancies him and when they get together they really enjoy each other's company. Luckily we don't see him that much, but being at a social event with him would be a challenge for me, without doubt.
Therapist [writing on board]:	OK, so I'll write down Philip. What's the other one?
Edwin:	Seeing my wife enjoy the company of an attractive guy while wearing her bikini, like at a beach or a by a pool. I must admit that I have refused to go away to places

(Continued)

(Continued)

	where she will wear her bikini, so we have city holidays and I avoid going swimming with her in hotel pools for the same reason. She hasn't twigged my avoidance strategy and I know she would be over the moon if I suggested a beach holiday.
Therapist [writing on board]:	OK. Anything else?
Edwin:	Not that comes to mind.
Therapist:	Anything else you are avoiding that might be a vulnerability factor?
Edwin:	Not that I can think of.
Therapist:	Can I suggest that as a homework assignment you give it more thought?
Edwin:	Deal.
Therapist:	And it may be that later you may encounter a factor that might prove to be a vulnerability factor. If so, let me know and we'll work on it.

[In her last few interventions the therapist is indicating that the list of vulnerability factors that they are compiling is a 'work in progress' and may need to be added to.]

Edwin:	OK.
Therapist:	OK, let's discuss a provisional order in which we need to deal with these vulnerability factors.
Edwin:	Well, the easiest is the internal sense of I've cracked it. Then, probably watching my wife talk to an attractive guy wearing a bikini. Philip would be the big one for me.
Therapist:	Should we deal with them in that order?
Edwin:	That would make sense.
Therapist:	We could always change the order later and incorporate other factors that you might come up with as needs be.

[Although it's not the case here, if a therapist thinks of factors that she thinks might be vulnerability factors for the client, she is free to put them forward for discussion.]

Encouraging the Client to Take the Lead in Assessing the Vulnerability Factor

At this point in the therapeutic process the client would have made progress in therapy at least on the target problem (in this case Edwin's jealousy). As such, the therapist should ideally be assuming more of a coaching stance (see Chapter 4, pp. 42–4) at this point. Consequently, the therapist is advised to encourage her client to take the lead in making an assessment of a target vulnerability factor (i.e. the factor that they have agreed to work on). Note how Edwin's therapist encourages him to do this.

Therapist:	OK, so let's see if we can understand what's going on when you think you've 'cracked it'. Why don't you take the lead in doing an ABC assessment on the factor and I'll help out if you get stuck. OK?
Edwin:	OK. Well, I guess my 'C' is behavioural because I have stopped working on my jealousy problem. Is that right?
Therapist:	Sounds good so far.
Edwin:	... But I'm struggling to find my 'A'.
Therapist:	The 'A' is a bit elusive. Try thinking of it as a condition that you think has to exist if you are to keep working on your problem.

[As the therapist notes, it is difficult for the Edwin to identify his 'A' because it is absent. Her question orients him to the important factor.]

Edwin:	I'm demanding that there has to be something I can't handle for me to keep working on it.
Therapist:	Can you question that demand?
Edwin:	Well, it's not true because I can keep working on my problem without the sense that I can't handle something. I can regard keeping working at it as like taking pills to keep my blood pressure down. The problems start when I don't do the work or take the pills.
Therapist:	Great work and I love the analogy.

Encouraging the Client to Rehearse Dealing with his Vulnerability Factor in Imagery

Before encouraging the client to practise dealing with a vulnerability factor in reality, especially when this factor is external to the client, it is useful to suggest that he rehearse dealing with it in imagery first, even when it is internal.

Therapist:	It's useful to deal with vulnerability factors in imagery before dealing with it when it occurs in reality, so can I suggest some imagery rehearsal?
Edwin:	OK.
Therapist:	Close your eyes and imagine that you find yourself thinking that you've cracked your jealousy problem. Can you imagine that?
Edwin:	I can.
Therapist:	Use that thought to rehearse the idea that you don't have to have the sense that you can't handle a jealousy-related scenario to continue to work at dealing with your jealousy issue. Let me know when you have that in your mind?
Edwin:	... OK. It's there.
Therapist:	Now see yourself continue to work at your problem while holding this belief and indicate when you have that clear in your mind.
Edwin:	OK ... it's clear.
Therapist:	Would rehearsing dealing with this vulnerability factor be useful?
Edwin:	Yes it would.
Therapist:	OK. We'll talk about that at the end of the session when we come to negotiate homework.

As the therapist notes, it is useful for the client to rehearse dealing with his vulnerability factor in imagery before confronting it in reality. Doing such imagery rehearsal about three times a day is to be recommended.

Encouraging the Client to Deal with his Vulnerability Factor in Reality

Once the client feels ready, he should be encouraged to deal with his vulnerability factor in reality. My view of such readiness is that the client should find dealing with the factor 'challenging, but not overwhelming', and consider that he can use the skills of dealing with the factor that he has been practising in imagery. If the client considers that facing the factor is too much for him at the present time, doing so should be postponed until it becomes a 'challenging, but not overwhelming' issue (Dryden, 1985).

The following dialogue takes place after Edwin has worked with his therapist on dealing with seeing his wife talk to an attractive guy while she is in her bikini. He has done two weeks' imagery work on the issue and is ready to face the factor in reality.

Therapist:	So you feel ready to confront this vulnerability factor in reality?
Edwin:	Ready as I'll ever be.
Therapist:	Logistically, how are you going to arrange it?
Edwin:	Well, as luck would have it there is a 'do' at our local gym this weekend to attract new members and it's swimming and drinks round the pool, so I suggested to Linda that we go and she is really looking forward to it.
Therapist:	So are you all prepared?
Edwin:	Yes, rational belief to the ready, behaviour all planned and strategies to deal with thinking, images and urges to act in place!
Therapist:	Let me make a suggestion. Have you seen the pool before?
Edwin:	No.
Therapist:	Why not go and visit it before the weekend so you can rehearse dealing with the vulnerability factor with the pool clearly in mind.
Edwin:	Great idea. I'll do that.

[The therapist makes this suggestion because the closer Edwin's image can reflect the reality of the context in which he is going to confront his vulnerability factor the better.]

Dealing with Client Lapses

As I pointed out earlier, clients will almost inevitably lapse while dealing with their problem at some point in the therapeutic process. How they deal with their lapses will influence their future therapeutic work and we know that clients who relapse often have either disturbed themselves about their lapses and/or have not learned from them.

Helping the Client to Deal with his Disturbance about Lapsing

When a client has experienced a lapse and has disturbed himself about the lapse, then the therapist needs to help the client deal with the disturbance before doing anything else. This is what Edwin's therapist did when Edwin indicated that he had disturbed himself about lapsing in an excerpt that I presented earlier in this chapter (see pp. 97–9).

Helping the Client to Learn from Lapsing

Once the therapist has helped the client to address his disturbance about his lapse, she needs to help him to understand why he lapsed in the first place. Putting the lapse episode into the ABC framework is a useful way of doing this, either formally or informally. It is useful where the client lapse is conceptualised as 'C'.

Thus, when the therapist looked with Edwin to see why he lapsed in the first place (at 'C'), it was because of his irrational belief (at 'B') about his urge when he felt it strongly (at 'A'). What he learned from this episode was that he can maintain a rational belief about an urge no matter how strong it is.

Normalising Lapsing and Helping the Client to Maintain the Commitment to Change

At some point in helping clients to deal with lapses, it is useful for the therapist to 'normalise' lapsing. This means explaining that lapsing is almost inevitable in the change process and, as such, it is a matter for self-acceptance and learning rather than self-depreciation and discouragement. The use of appropriate metaphors and aphorisms is useful here (e.g. 'Giving up smoking is easy. I've done it hundreds of times' – Mark Twain), as is relevant therapist self-disclosure.

Helping the Client Deal with the Fear of Relapse

Sometimes in doing relapse prevention work, the client reveals an anxiety of relapse that, if not dealt with, serves as a vulnerability factor for relapse. As such, it is important that the therapist helps the client deal with it. There are two ways of helping the client deal with relapse anxiety.

Treating relapse as a cognitive 'C'

When a therapist treats relapse as a cognitive 'C', she conceptualises it as a thinking consequence of an irrational belief about a prior 'A'. This most often occurs with clients who have demands about being in self-control. Here is a typical client ABC in this area:

Situation: The client lapses
A: This lapse means that I am not in full self-control.
B: I must be in self-control and it's terrible if I'm not.
C (emotional): Anxiety
   (thinking):   'I will relapse'

The therapeutic task here is for the therapist to help the client to develop and rehearse a rational belief about lapsing and to be more flexible about self-control. In doing so, the therapist helps the client to think in a more balanced way about the chances of him experiencing a relapse based on the data at hand and the work that he can do to help himself deal effectively with lapses.

Treating relapse as an 'A'

Because it is always possible for a client to experience a relapse, and particularly when the previous strategy has not alleviated the client's relapse anxiety, the therapist is advised to encourage the client to assume the worst and imagine that he does relapse. The therapeutic task here is to encourage the client to think rationally about relapse and, in particular, to take the horror out of relapse, but not the badness out of it.

Once the therapist helps the client to think rationally about lapses in self-control and relapse itself, then the client is duly concerned about it happening, but not unduly anxious about it. When this happens, this issue ceases to serve as a vulnerability factor for the client.

Dealing with Relapse

Sometimes the worst does happen and the client does 'go back to square one' and relapses. What is the therapist to do in such a situation? The most important thing that the therapist can do is to convey a calm response and not get discouraged herself. The client is likely to be feeling discouraged and the last thing he needs is a discouraged therapist. So if the therapist is feeling that way, then she needs to identify, examine and change any irrational beliefs that may be at the root of her discouragement.

While therapist calmness and encouragement are important factors, they are far from sufficient to help the client deal productively with relapse. The skilful, calm and encouraging therapist needs to demonstrate her skills in the following areas.

Help the Client to Deal with his Disturbance about Relapse

Since relapse is a significant adversity, the client is likely to disturb himself about relapsing. If this is the case, the first thing the therapist needs to do is to help the client deal effectively with his disturbed feelings using the skills of examining beliefs that I dealt with earlier in this chapter (see pp. 86–93). At an appropriate time during this belief examination phase, I sometimes tell the client the following story:

> In the late 1990s I wrote a book entitled *Overcoming Shame* (Dryden, 1997) on a portable word-processor. Once I had written the book, I transferred the chapters from the machine's internal memory to a floppy disk, a procedure I had done many times. Because I needed to use the machine for another project, I cleared the internal memory. When I came to print out the book from the floppy disk it wasn't there! I was sure that

I had done something wrong, but did not know what. I demanded that I absolutely should not have made such a stupid error and was furious with myself. Effectively, I was disturbing myself for experiencing a relapse since I was back to square one with the book. After a period of self-fury and kicking various items of furniture, I reminded myself that I was an REBT therapist and resolved to use my REBT skills on myself. So this is what I did and I calmed myself to the point that I was very disappointed that I had made such a stupid error, which resulted in me losing my book, but I was no longer furious with myself for doing so.

Helping the Client to Learn From Relapse

Once the client has undisturbed himself about relapsing, the therapist's task is to help him learn from the relapse. What did he do and not do that contributed to his relapse. The chances are, as I have said before, that he did not deal effectively with previous lapses and/or failed to cope with one or more vulnerability factor(s). If so, the therapist should work with the client to review these past events to make a future plan to implement what he has learned from his previous errors.

During this phase, I continue my story as follows:

After I had worked to undisturb myself about the stupid mistake that I must have done to end up with no book, I read the machine's manual and realised what I did. In naming the chapter files, I had inserted a full-stop, which meant that the files could not be copied on to a floppy disk. I had lost my book because of eight full stops! I resolved not to do that again and to read the user manual more thoroughly before doing any other procedures that might jeopardise my material.

Helping the Client to Choose between Renewing his Commitment to Change or to Stay in a Relapsed State

After the client has undisturbed himself about relapsing and the therapist has helped him to learn from the relapse and to develop a future plan based on that learning, the therapist then needs to help the client to see that he has a choice: to renew a commitment to change or to stay with his problem. It is here that the therapist elicits and deals with a range of client doubts, reservations or objections (DROs) about his own capacity for change and REBT's suitability to help him change.

With respect to the client's DROs about his own capacity, it is likely that behind these DROs lies a set of irrational beliefs in the area of discomfort disturbance (see Chapter 1). Helping the client to identify, examine and change these irrational beliefs is the therapist's major task here as well as encouraging him to take one day at a time to see how things go.

Concerning REBT's suitability to help the client, it is important to help the client be more specific about this since doing so often unearths misconceptions that the client still holds about the approach. Dealing with these misconceptions in the manner described earlier in this chapter (see pp. 102–3) is what the skilful REBT therapist does in such situations.

However, it may be that REBT may not be best suited to the client, and if this is the case, the therapist might suggest that the client try a different approach with the understanding that he can resume REBT with the therapist if he so chooses.

I conclude my own story in this phase, as follows:

> After my salutary experience with the full stops and having read the user manual from cover to cover, I had a stark choice: To write the book from scratch or not. Although it seemed daunting, I decided to start the book again, write for a week and then review my decision. This is what I did. After a week I was well into the book and decided to continue. When I finished the book, I was very careful to transfer the chapters to the floppy disk ... with success and the book was published nine months later!

After telling the client my story I initiate a discussion concerning what he can learn from my experience.

Ending Therapy

In some ways, I rarely end therapy formally with any of my clients unless they move away from the area, and even then, I have been known to do the occasional session with a client who has moved abroad. While this may seem a shocking statement, I look at it this way. I do not go to my GP and say to him at the end of a consultation 'Thank you for all your help, this is the last time I will be seeing you', unless of course I am moving out of his catchment area.

In the same way, my door is always open for any clients to consult me should they need to do so. This should be viewed within the context that I and my REBT colleagues work to make ourselves redundant as quickly as we can, and strive to encourage our clients to become their own therapists by taking increasing responsibility for maintaining the changes that we have helped them to initiate. To aid this process we gradually wind down, taking an active-directive stance with them and increasingly adopt a coaching stance (see Chapter 4, pp. 37–44 for a discussion of these two stances).

Even when clients say that they want to end therapy, I would frequently indicate that my door is open to them should they wish to return. I say that because it reflects reality. Some of my psychodynamic colleagues say that REBT therapists adopt this stance towards ending therapy because we want to defend ourselves against the pain of ending therapy with our clients or against our pain of dealing with our clients' pain about ending. While I cannot say definitively that they are wrong, I doubt that this is the case. Our position on ending therapy is very much influenced by our practice of working with our clients to consult us less frequently as they make progress since our emphasis is on encouraging them to be their own therapists.

Having made the REBT position clear on endings, let me outline certain issues that are relevant to this subject.

1   The REBT therapist encourages the client to become his own therapist as early as feasible by moving from taking an active-directive stance to a coaching stance.
2   When the therapist and client decide that the client is ready, the gap between sessions is gradually increased.
3   When they both agree, a time is set for the client to end therapy (with the understanding that the door is open should he wish to return).
4   Towards the end of therapy, the therapist helps the client to review what he has achieved and learned from therapy.
5   The therapist agrees criteria with the client for him to contact the therapist in the future (normally after the client has made a concerted effort to help himself, which has failed, or when he is facing a new issue that he can't deal with on his own).
6   The therapist plans a future review session to monitor client progress.
7   The therapist gives the client an opportunity to raise and discuss any unfinished business.
8   The therapist gives the client an opportunity to work through issues to do with ending and with dealing with life without therapy and the therapist. It is here that mutual feelings of sadness and appreciation are generally expressed.

Tasks and the Working Alliance

In closing this chapter let me reiterate that an important way of looking at the therapist's tasks in REBT is within the framework of the working alliance. When that framework is employed, several points that I first discussed in Chapter 3 need to be implemented by the REBT therapist. Thus, it is important that the therapist:

1   Helps her client understand the nature of his tasks (i.e. the client's) in REBT.
2   Helps the client understand the instrumental value of doing his tasks in REBT and that if he does them, then he will increase the chances of reaching his therapeutic goals.
3   Ensures that the client has the ability to execute his tasks in REBT and does not ask him to do things that are beyond his ability.
4   Ensures that the client has the skills to execute his tasks in REBT and if not, she should teach him these skills.
5   Helps the client by inspiring him with the confidence that he can do the assignment.
6   Ensures that the client only uses techniques in REBT that have sufficient potency to enable him to achieve his goals.
7   Needs to help the client to understand the nature of his therapist's tasks and how they can help him to achieve his goals.

If these points are skilfully implemented in REBT, then the therapist will have fulfilled much of her responsibility in the therapeutic process.

However, the client also has responsibility in this process and thus, while this book is not about clients' skills in REBT, it is useful to close this book by emphasising that it takes two to do the therapeutic tango and that while the therapist may have super-skills, if the client does not operationalise his responsibility for self-change, then he won't change. Thus, when I am asked if REBT and CBT work, my reply is 'Yes, if both therapist and client do their respective jobs and no if they don't!'

Thus, in REBT, the client needs to:

1   Disclose his problems to the therapist as honestly as possible.
2   Be open to the REBT framework and give his informed consent to proceed if this framework makes sense to him.
3   Disclose his doubts, reservations and objections about REBT theory and practice to his therapist.
4   Put into practice outside therapy what he learns in therapy.
5   Take responsibility for applying REBT self-change skills after therapy.

We have now reached the end of the book. I hope you have found it useful and I welcome feedback c/o the publisher.

APPENDIX 1: WHAT IS RATIONAL EMOTIVE BEHAVIOUR THERAPY (REBT)?

An example of material sent to prospective clients or to clients who have made a first appointment that outlines the REBT view of psychological problems and how it addresses these problems (Dryden, 2006b).

What is Rational Emotive Behaviour Therapy (REBT)?

I practise a form of counselling known as Rational Emotive Behaviour Therapy (REBT). It is one of the cognitive-behaviour therapies currently in vogue. REBT is based on an old idea attributed to Epictetus, a Roman philosopher, who said that 'Men are disturbed not by things, but by their views of things'. In REBT, we have modified this and say that 'People are disturbed not by things, but by their rigid and extreme views of things'. Once they have disturbed themselves they then try to get rid of their disturbed feelings in ways that ultimately serve to maintain their problems.

As an REBT therapist I will help you to identify, examine and change the rigid and extreme beliefs that we argue underpin your emotional problems and help you to develop alternative flexible and non-extreme beliefs. I will also help you to examine the ways in which you have tried to help yourself that haven't worked and encourage you to develop and practise more effective, durable strategies. At the beginning of counselling, together we will consider your problems one at a time and I will teach you a framework which will help you to break down your problems one by one into their constituent parts. I will also teach you a variety of methods for examining and changing your rigid and extreme beliefs and a variety of methods to help you to consolidate and strengthen your alternative flexible and non-extreme beliefs. As therapy proceeds, I will help you to take increasing responsibility for using these methods and my ultimate aim is to help you to become your own therapist. As this happens, we will meet less frequently until you feel you can cope on your own.

APPENDIX 2: USING THE 'MONEY MODEL' TO EXPLAIN THE REBT MODEL OF PSYCHOLOGICAL DISTURBANCE

An Example of Dr Albert Ellis Using the 'Money Model' to Explain the REBT Model of Psychological Disturbance (Ellis & Dryden, 1997: 40–1)

Ellis: Imagine that you prefer to have a minimum of $11 in your pocket at all times, but it's not necessary that you have this amount. If you discover you only have $10, how will you feel?

Client: Frustrated.

Ellis: Right. Or you'd feel concerned or sad, but you wouldn't kill yourself. Right?

Client: Right.

Ellis: OK. Now this time imagine that you absolutely *have to* have a minimum $11 in your pocket at all times. You *must* have it, it is a *necessity*. You *must*, you *must*, you *must* have a minimum of $11, and again you look and you find you only have $10. How will you feel?

Client: Very anxious.

Ellis: Right, or depressed. Now remember it's the same $10, but a different belief. OK, now this time you still have the same belief. You *have to* have a minimum of $11 at all times, you *must*. It's absolutely *essential*. But this time you look in your pocket and find that you've got $15. How will you feel?

Client: Relieved, content.

Ellis: Right. But with that same belief, you *have to* have a minimum of $11 at all times – something will occur to you to scare you shitless. What do you think that would be?

Client: What if I lose $5?

Ellis: Right. What if I lose $5, what if I spend $5, what if I get robbed? That's right. Now the moral of this model – which applies to just about all humans, rich or poor, black or white, male or female, young or old, in the past or in the future, assuming humans are still human – is that people *make themselves* miserable if they don't get what they think they *must* get, but they are also panicked when they do get what they think they *must* get – because of the must. For even if they have what they think they must have, they could always lose it.

Client: So I have no chance to be happy when I don't have what I think I *must* have – and little chance of remaining unanxious when I do have it?

Ellis: Right! Your *must*urbation will get you nowhere – except depressed or panicked!

From Ellis, A. and Dryden, W. (1997). *The Practice of Rational Emotive Behaviour Therapy*, 2nd edn, Chapter 2: The Basic Principles of REBT. New York: Springer, pp. 40–1. Reproduced in modified form with the permission of Springer Publishing Co., LLC, New York, NY 10036.

APPENDIX 3: A TABULAR SUMMARY OF UNHEALTHY NEGATIVE EMOTIONS IN REBT

Emotion	Inference[1] in relation to personal domain[2]	Type of belief	Cognitive consequences	Action tendencies
Anxiety[3] (ego or discomfort)	• Threat of danger	Irrational	• Overestimates probability of threat occurring • Underestimates ability to cope with the threat • Creates an even more negative threat in one's mind • Has more task-irrelevant thoughts than in concern	• To withdraw physically from the threat • To withdraw mentally from the threat • To ward off the threat (e.g. by superstitious behaviour) • To tranquilise feelings • To seek reassurance
Depression[4] (ego or discomfort)	• Loss (with implications for future) • Failure	Irrational	• Sees only negative aspects of the loss or failure. • Thinks of other losses and failures that one has experienced • Thinks one is unable to help self (helplessness) • Only sees pain and blackness in the future (hopelessness)	• To withdraw from reinforcements • To withdraw into oneself • To create an environment consistent with feelings • To attempt to terminate feelings of depression in self-destructive ways
Unhealthy anger	• Frustration • Goal obstruction • Self or other transgresses personal rule • Threat to self-esteem	Irrational	• Overestimates the extent to which the other person acted deliberately • Sees malicious intent in the motives of others • Self seen as definitely right; other(s) seen as definitely wrong • Unable to see the other person's point of view • Plots to exact revenge	• To attack the other physically • To attack other verbally • To attack the other passive-aggressively • To displace the attack on to another person, animal or object • To withdraw aggressively • To recruit allies against the other

Emotion	Inference[1] in relation to personal domain[2]	Type of belief	Cognitive consequences	Action tendencies
Guilt	• Violation of moral code (sin of commission) • Failure to live up to moral code (sin of omission) • Hurts the feelings of a significant other	Irrational	• Assumes that one has definitely committed the sin • Assumes more personal responsibility than the situation warrants • Assigns far less responsibility to others than is warranted • Does not think of mitigating factors • Does not put behaviour into overall context • Thinks that one will receive retribution	• To escape from the unhealthy pain of guilt in self-defeating ways • To beg forgiveness from the person wronged • To promise unrealistically that one will not 'sin' again • To punish self physically or by deprivation • To disclaim responsibility for wrongdoing • To reject offers of forgiveness
Shame	• Something shameful has been revealed about self (or group with whom one identifies) by self or others • Acting in a way that falls very short of ione's deal • Others will look down on or shun self (or group with whom one identifies)	Irrational	• Overestimates the 'shamefulness' of the information revealed • Overestimates the likelihood that the judging group will notice or be interested in the information • Overestimates the degree of disapproval self (or reference group) will receive • Overestimates the length of time any disapproval will last	• To remove self from the 'gaze' of others • To isolate self from others • To save face by attacking other(s) who have 'shamed' self • To defend threatened self-esteem in self-defeating ways • To ignore attempts by others to restore social equilibrium

(Continued)

(Continued)

Emotion	Inference[1] in relation to personal domain[2]	Type of belief	Cognitive consequences	Action tendencies
Hurt	• Other treats self badly (self undeserving)	Irrational	• Overestimates the unfairness of the other person's behaviour • Other perceived as showing lack of care or as indifferent • Self seen as alone, uncared for or misunderstood • Tends to think of past 'hurts' • Expects other to make the first move toward repairing relationship	• To shut down communication channel with the other • To sulk and make obvious one is hurt without disclosing details of the matter • To indirectly criticise or punish the other for the offence
Unhealthy jealousy	• Threat to relationship with partner from another person	Irrational	• Tends to see threats to one's relationship when none really exists • Thinks the loss of one's relationship is imminent • Misconstrues one's partner's ordinary conversations as having romantic or sexual connotations • Constructs visual images of partner's infidelity • If partner admits to finding another attractive, believes that the other is seen as more attractive than self and that one's partner will leave self for this other person	• To seek constant reassurance that one is loved • To monitor the actions the feelings of one's partner • To search for evidence that one's partner is involved with someone else • To attempt to restrict the movements or activities of one's partner • To set tests which partner has to pass • To retaliate for partner's presumed infidelity • To sulk

Emotion	Inference[1] in relation to personal domain[2]	Type of belief	Cognitive consequences	Action tendencies
Unhealthy envy	• Another person possesses and enjoys something desirable that the person does not have	Irrational	• Tends to denigrate the value of the desired possession and/or the person who possesses it • Tries to convince self that one is happy with one's possessions (although one is not) • Thinks about how to acquire the desired possession regardless of its usefulness • Thinks about how to deprive the other person of the desired possession • Thinks about how to spoil or destroy the other's desired possession	• To disparage verbally the person who has the desired possession • To disparage verbally the desired possession • To take away the desired possession from the other (either so that one will have it or the other is deprived of it) • To spoil or destroy the desired possession so that the other person does not have it

Notes

1 Inference = Personally significant hunch that goes beyond observable reality and which gives meaning to it: may be accurate or inaccurate.

2 Personal domain = The objects – tangible and intangible – in which a person has an involvement (Beck, 1976). REBT theory distinguishes between ego and comfort aspects of the personal domain, although those aspects frequently interact.

3 REBT theory distinguishes between ego anxiety and discomfort anxiety.

4 Depression in this context refers to non-clinical depression.

I wish to thank Join Wiley & Sons Ltd for allowing me to use part of Figure 4.1 in Windy Dryden and Rhena Branch (2008) *The Fundamentals of Rational Emotive Behaviour Therapy: A Training Handbook*, 2nd edn. Chichester: Wiley, Copyright John Wiley & Sons Ltd. Reproduced with permission.

REFERENCES

Barker, C., Pistrang, N., Shapiro, D.A., & Shaw, I. (1990). Coping and help-seeking in the UK adult population. *British Journal of Clinical Psychology, 29,* 271–85.

Beck, A.T. (1976). *Cognitive therapy and the emotional disorders.* New York: International Universities Press.

Beck, A.T., Rush, A.J., Shaw, B.F., & Emery, G. (1979). *Cognitive therapy of depression.* New York: Guilford Press.

Bernard, M.E., & Wolfe, J.L. (Eds.). (1993). *The RET resource book for practitioners.* New York: Albert Ellis Institute.

Bordin, E.S. (1979). The generalizability of the psychoanalytic concept of the working alliance. *Psychotherapy: Theory, Research and Practice, 16*(3), 252–60.

Burns, D.D., & Spangler, D.L. (2000). Does psychotherapy homework lead to improvements in depression in cognitive–behavioral therapy or does improvement lead to increased homework compliance? *Journal of Consulting and Clinical Psychology, 68,* 46–56.

DiGiuseppe, R. (1991). Comprehensive cognitive disputing in rational-emotive therapy. In M. Bernard (Ed.), *Using rational–emotive therapy effectively.* New York: Plenum.

Dorn, F.J. (Ed.). (1984). *The social influence process in counseling and psychotherapy.* Springfield, IL: Charles C. Thomas.

Dryden, W. (1985). Challenging but not overwhelming: A compromise in negotiating homework assignments. *British Journal of Cognitive Psychotherapy, 3*(1), 77–80.

Dryden, W. (1986). A case of theoretically consistent eclecticism: Humanizing a computer 'addict'. *International Journal of Eclectic Psychotherapy, 5*(4), 309–27.

Dryden, W. (1987). *Current issues in rational-emotive therapy.* London: Croom Helm.

Dryden, W. (1989). The therapeutic alliance as an integrating framework. In W. Dryden (Ed.), *Key issues for counselling in action.* London: Sage.

Dryden, W. (1997). *Overcoming shame.* London: Sheldon Press.

Dryden, W. (1998). Understanding persons in the context of their problems: A rational emotive behaviour therapy perspective. In M. Bruch & F.W. Bond (Eds.), *Beyond diagnosis: Case formulation approaches in CBT.* Chichester: John Wiley & Sons.

Dryden, W. (1999). *How to accept yourself.* London: Sheldon Press.

Dryden, W. (2001). *Reason to change: A rational emotive behaviour therapy (REBT) workbook.* Hove, East Sussex: Brunner-Routledge.

Dryden, W. (2004). *Rational emotive behaviour therapy: Clients' manual.* London: Whurr.

Dryden, W. (2006a). *Getting started with REBT: A concise guide for clients.* Hove, East Sussex: Routledge.

Dryden, W. (2006b). *Counselling in a nutshell.* London: Sage.

Dryden, W. (2008). *Rational emotive behaviour therapy: Distinctive features*. London: Routledge.

Dryden, W. (2009a). *Understanding emotional problems: An REBT perspective*. London: Routledge.

Dryden, W. (2009b). *How to think and intervene like an REBT therapist*. London: Routledge.

Dryden, W., & Branch, R. (2008). *The fundamentals of rational emotive behaviour therapy: a training handbook*, 2nd edn. Chichestes: John Wiley & Sons.

Dryden, W., & Neenan, M. (2004a). *The rational emotive behavioural approach to therapeutic change*. London: Sage.

Dryden, W., & Neenan, M. (2004b). *Counselling individuals: A rational emotive behavioural handbook*. London: Whurr.

Ellis, A. (1959). Requisite conditions for basic personality change. *Journal of Consulting Psychology, 23*, 538–40.

Ellis, A. (1962). *Reason and emotion in psychotherapy*. Secaucus, NJ: Lyle Stuart.

Ellis, A. (1963). Toward a more precise definition of 'emotional' and 'intellectual' insight. *Psychological Reports, 13*, 125–6.

Ellis, A. (1976). The biological basis of human irrationality. *Journal of Individual Psychology, 32*, 145–86.

Ellis, A. (1980). The value of efficiency in psychotherapy. *Psychotherapy: Theory, Research and Practice, 17*, 414–18.

Ellis, A. (1983). The philosophic implications and dangers of some popular behavior therapy techniques. In M. Rosenbaum, C.M. Franks, & Y. Jaffe (Eds), *Perspectives in behavior therapy in the eighties*. New York: Springer.

Ellis, A. (1994). *Reason and emotion in psychotherapy*, Revised and updated edn. New York: Birch Lane Press.

Ellis, A. (2002). *Overcoming resistance: A rational emotive behavior therapy integrated approach*, 2nd edn. New York: Springer.

Ellis, A., & Dryden, W. (1997). *The practice of rational emotive behavior therapy*, 2nd edn. New York: Springer.

Emmelkamp, P.M.G., Kuipers, A.C.M., & Eggeraat, J.B. (1978). Cognitive modification versus prolonged exposure in vivo: A comparison with agoraphobics as subjects. *Behaviour Research and Therapy, 16*, 33–41.

Garvin, C.D., & Seabury, B.A. (1997). *Interpersonal practice in social work: Promoting competence and social competence*, 2nd edn. Boston, MA: Allyn & Bacon.

Gilbert, P., & Leahy, R.L. (Eds.). (2007). *The therapeutic relationship in the cognitive-behavioural therapies*. London: Routledge.

Grieger, R.M., & Woods, P.J. (1998). *Rational-emotive therapy companion: A clear, concise, and complete guide to being an RET client*. Roanoke, VA: Scholars Press.

Hjelle, L.A., & Ziegler, D.J. (1992). *Personality theories: Basic assumptions, research and applications*. New York: McGraw-Hill.

Joyce, J., & Sills, C. (2001). *Skills in gestalt counselling and psychotherapy*. London: Sage.

Lazarus, A.A. (1973). 'Hypnosis' as a facilitator in behavior therapy. *International Journal of Clinical and Experimental Hypnosis, 21*, 25–31.

Lazarus, A.A. (1981). *The practice of multimodal therapy*. New York: McGraw-Hill.

Lister-Ford, C. (2002). *Skills in transactional analysis and psychotherapy*. London: Sage.

Luborsky, L., McLellan, A.T., Woody, G.E., O'Brien, C.P., & Auerbach, A. (1985). Therapist success and its determinants. *Archives of General Psychiatry, 42*, 602–11.

Marlatt, G.A., & Donovan, D.M. (Eds.). (2005). *Relapse prevention: Maintenance strategies in the treatment of addictive behaviors,* 2nd edn. New York: Guilford Press.

Neenan, M., & Dryden, W. (1996). *Dealing with difficulties in rational emotive behaviour therapy.* London: Whurr.

Neenan, M., & Dryden, W. (1999). *Rational emotive behaviour therapy: Advances in theory and practice.* London: Whurr.

Pistrang, N., & Barker, C. (1992). Clients' beliefs about psychological problems. *Counselling Psychology Quarterly, 5,* 325–36.

Rogers, C.R. (1957). The necessary and sufficient conditions of therapeutic personality change. *Journal of Consulting Psychology, 21,* 95–103.

Salovey, P. (Ed.). (1991). *The psychology of jealousy and envy.* New York: Guilford Press.

Tolan, J. (2003). *Skills in person-centred counselling and psychotherapy.* London: Sage.

Wessler, R.A., & Wessler, R.L. (1980). *The principles and practice of rational–emotive therapy.* San Francisco: Jossey-Bass.

Wills, F. (2008). *Skills in cognitive behaviour counselling and psychotherapy.* London: Sage.

Woods, P. (1991). Orthodox RET taught effectively with graphics, feedback on irrational beliefs, a structured homework series and models of disputation. In M.E. Bernard (Ed.), *Using rational-emotive therapy effectively: A practitioner's guide.* New York: Plenum.

Ziegler, D.J. (2000). Basic assumptions concerning human nature underlying rational emotive behaviour therapy (REBT) personality theory. *Journal of Rational-Emotive and Cognitive-Behavior Therapy, 18,* 67–85.

INDEX

Note: Page numbers in *italic* refer to figures and diagrams

Supporting researchers for more than forty years

Research methods have always been at the core of SAGE's publishing. Sara Miller McCune founded SAGE in 1965 and soon after, she published SAGE's first methods book, Public Policy Evaluation. A few years later, she launched the Quantitative Applications in the Social Sciences series – affectionately known as the "little green books".

Always at the forefront of developing and supporting new approaches in methods, SAGE published early groundbreaking texts and journals in the fields of qualitative methods and evaluation.

Today, more than forty years and two million little green books later, SAGE continues to push the boundaries with a growing list of more than 1,200 research methods books, journals, and reference works across the social, behavioral, and health sciences.

From qualitative, quantitative, mixed methods to evaluation, SAGE is the essential resource for academics and practitioners looking for the latest methods by leading scholars.

www.sagepublications.com